REAL ESTATE
DUE DILIGENCE

THE INVESTOR'S GUIDE TO
AVOIDING COSTLY MISTAKES

JOE TORRE

REAL ESTATE DUE DILIGENCE:
The Investor's Guide to Avoiding Costly Mistakes
by Joe Torre
1. BUS054010 2. BUS050020 3. BUS054000
ISBN: 978-1-949642-64-3
EBOOK: 978-1-949642-65-0

Cover design by LEWIS AGRELL

Printed in the United States of America

Authority Publishing
11230 Gold Express Dr. #310-413
Gold River, CA 95670
800-877-1097
www.AuthorityPublishing.com

DEDICATION

Geraldine Barry
(1964 – 2019)

To Geraldine Barry,
real estate mentor and friend, who left us too early.

ACKNOWLEDGEMENTS

Writing a book is a lot more work than I expected and would not have been possible without the support of some seasoned investors and industry veterans who provided great feedback and suggestions that added clarity and completeness to the final version. They include:

Natasha Keck
Kay Gunderson
Elizabeth Macken
Graham Parham
Michelle Pepper

I must also thank my proofreader George Mason (gbm6345@gmail.com) and the team at Authority Publishing for guiding me through the process and protecting me from things I didn't know I didn't know.

Of course, any remaining mistakes or omissions remain mine, alone.

CONTENTS

PART II
SPECIAL SITUATIONS

INTRODUCTION

If you follow the guidelines in this book to the letter, you will never buy an investment property in your lifetime. That's because no single investment property will "check all the boxes" and provide the ideal investment that we all want: One that both cash flows and appreciates, one that was purchased below market, has no risk, has tenants who never leave, and makes you money until the end of time.

In the real world, there are tradeoffs. For instance, you may want a brand-new property in a good school district, but that property will likely be too expensive to cash flow. Or you may want a property that offers great cash flow but is in a less-desirable neighborhood with more crime and lower-quality tenants.

You can't have it all, and part of this book is about understanding the tradeoffs and deciding where and how you want to place your bets.

WHY I WROTE THIS BOOK

I work full-time as an Investment Counselor for a real estate investment firm, and I've seen a lot of investors make a lot of mistakes over the years, including me. It's easy to make an expensive mistake by missing one small detail, and no investor can be aware of every potential pitfall. Conversely, I've seen investors who suffer from "analysis paralysis": They're paranoid about what key factor they might be missing and so they read books and attend seminars for years but never "pull the trigger."

Each chapter in this book covers a large enough topic to warrant a book of its own. While I can't include everything there is to know about each topic, I believe provide enough to enable you to make your own investment decisions and ask the right questions of the people you work with.

My goal is to "tell it like it is"—the way I'd want someone to tell me if I were starting out. This book provides the analytical tools for single-family home investors like you, so you can get past "analysis paralysis," do proper due diligence, and confidently build a portfolio of investment properties that helps you meet your financial goals.

FOCUS

There are a lot of investing strategies out there: flipping houses vs. buy-and-hold, new construction vs. existing, and others. For the most part, this book is for buy-and-hold investors, whether buying on your own, through a turnkey provider, or through a new home builder.

HOW TO READ THIS BOOK

Throughout the book, you'll see little icons or sidebars that add color to the discussion, e.g.:

Exception

The principles outlined in this book are sound but should not be applied robotically. As an investor, you should incorporate general principles but be aware that there may be exceptions to the rule, which if recognized, will enable you to take advantage of opportunities other investors pass up. I will give examples of exceptions to the rule, so you can feel more comfortable bending the rules in real life.

War Story

I will occasionally offer a real-world *War Story* to illustrate potential pitfalls, based on my experience.

Tip

Periodically I'll insert a *Tip* that will help you invest smarter or with less risk.

Extra for Experts

Sometimes I will delve into a topic in more detail than is needed by most readers; I will identify these tangents with an *Extra for Experts* heading. The reader can choose whether to skip over these sections or not.

Dogma Alert!

In general, I attempt to stick to the facts and leave my personal opinions and biases out of the discussion, but sometimes I feel the need to add my two cents. When I deviate from strictly factual presentations, I will warn you with this symbol: *Dogma Alert!* You'll then know that what follows is my personal opinion only, and not to be taken as gospel truth. Caveat emptor!

GLOSSARY

There are many terms used throughout the book (like "turn-key"). Their definitions can be found in Appendix A – Glossary. I recommend you scan that section before reading the book.

A Word about Pronouns

The English language has no gender-neutral pronoun for a single person, as some other languages do. English requires authors to write "he or she" or "s/he" when referring to either or both genders. I find this awkward and unwieldy.

Throughout this book I'll use the pronoun that, in my experience, is the most common for the context. For example, most electrical and plumbing contractors I've met are men. Actually, all of them were. Most property managers and leasing agents I've met are women. So when discussing these various players in the real estate world, I will be using "he" or "she" according to my experience.

Legal Disclaimer

Finally, to appease the attorneys, I must state that the views expressed in this book are those of the author alone, and do not in any way constitute investing advice. I don't know you or your situation, so I can't presume to offer you advice. Everyone has unique circumstances, goals, and risk tolerances, so you should consult your CPA or financial planner to get advice tailored to your unique situation. All investing involves risk and reading a 200-page guide on the subject does not remove your risk.

Joe Torre
February 2021

PART I

FUNDAMENTALS
OF
DUE DILIGENCE

CHAPTER 1

CHOOSING YOUR INVESTMENT STRATEGY

The first thing you have to do as an investor is decide on your investing strategy and your investing goals.

INVESTING MODELS

There are numerous ways to invest in real estate and all have their pros and cons. Here I'll discuss three of the most popular investing strategies for building your personal portfolio:

- Flipping
- Buy-and-hold through the BRRRR model
- Buy-and-hold either through a turnkey provider or new construction

Flipping

Flipping has been made popular in recent years by some popular TV shows. It basically involves buying a house in need of repair ("fixer-upper"), either personally renovating it or hiring work crews to renovate it, and then selling it for a gain.

Typical numbers would look like this: You buy a distressed property for $200,000, put $50,000 in renovations into it, and sell it for $300,000 for a gain of $50,000. The gain is usually less than projected because you'll have to pay holding costs like insurance and property taxes, or the rehab might cost more or take longer than you planned, or you may have vandalism. But even if you clear only $30,000 per deal, and do one deal per quarter, that's still $120,000 per year.

Keys to Success

1. Buy the worst house in the best neighborhood. If you can buy a "C" property in an "A" or "B" neighborhood, then renovate the property to the standard of the neighborhood, you can achieve outsize returns. The key to this strategy is to have good sources of inventory: bank foreclosure departments, wholesalers, or "bird dogs" (people who look for and identify properties with investment potential).

2. You need access to private lenders or hard-money lenders, as banks will not lend on distressed properties and you're not going to be holding it for 30 years anyway.

3. Solid, reliable work crews that don't rip you off.

4. Operating in a market where prices are rising is a big help. If your rehab budget has a cost overrun, rising home prices can help cover your overages.

Pros

- Potential for healthy gains.

- Good for investors who are handy.

Cons

- High risk: What you lose on one bad deal can erase what you gained on several good deals.

- Inventory is hard to come by and you're competing with many other flippers in most markets.

- No more free time: You've basically taken on a full-time job.

The BRRRR Model

Another strategy that's become popular in the last few years is called the BRRRR model, which stands for Buy, Renovate, Rent, Refi, Repeat. The following example is how it would work ideally.

Let's say you start out with $80,000 in your bank account. You buy a fixer-upper for all-cash for $60,000 and put $20,000 of renovations into it for a total all-in cost of $80,000. You then rent it out to a tenant and, after six months, you refinance the house with a conventional lender.

Here's the kicker: You didn't just pick any property; you strategically picked a property suitable for upgrading. Maybe you bought a three-bedroom, one-bath house and converted it into a three-bedroom, two-bath house, or a four-bedroom, two-bath house.

The fact that you added a bedroom and/or an extra bath is key, because after the renovation, your house is no longer valued at $80,000; it's worth $100,000 because you strategically upgraded it and increased its value.

Your lender only expects you to have 20% skin in the game (like a 20% down payment), so when you refinance, you get your original $80,000 back! You started with $80,000, and you ended with $80,000, plus an upgraded house! It feels like you got the house for free, but in fact you simply added value to it.

Then you take your $80,000 and do it again with another property. If you can do this once a year, you can churn your original $80,000 into a portfolio of multiple properties over time.

If it works as planned, BRRRR can be a powerful tool for building your wealth. But of course, things don't always go as planned. Maybe the After-Repair-Value (ARV) is only $90,000 so you can only get $72,000 (80% x $90,000) back from your refinance. Even then, you've got forced equity in your property and can add in some additional funds if needed to do your next deal.

Tip

It helps if you're operating in a market that's appreciating, because a rising market will help force the appreciation you're counting on to get your original capital back.

Buy-and-Hold

The buy-and-hold investing strategy is when you buy a property, either off Multiple Listing Services (MLS), from a new-home builder, or through a turnkey provider (more on that in the next chapter) with the intention of renting it out for a number of years or perhaps indefinitely.

This approach doesn't take as much time as the others and is great for people who have busy day jobs already and prefer a less aggressive and work-intensive approach.

Exhibit 1.1: Summary of Most Popular Business Models

	Flipping	BRRRR	Buy-and-Hold
Risk	High	Medium	Low
Time Commitment	High	Medium	Low
Potential for Built-in Equity	High	Medium-High	Low
Ongoing Maintenance	None	Low	Low-Medium
Pros	Don't have to deal with tenants or property managers	Can get appreciation quickly	Doesn't take as much time investment
Cons	No ongoing income. To keep earning, you have to do more deals so it's like having a job.	Works well in theory; in practice it's harder to find good enough deals on a regular basis.	No immediate equity but is good for building long-term wealth.
Skills Needed as an Investor	- Handyman - Manage work crews - Raise private money	- Find good sources of suitable properties - Manage work crews - Raise private money - Property Management	- Ability to pick markets and a good property manager - Ability to qualify for a home loan

INVESTING GOALS

Broadly speaking, there are three types of real estate markets you can invest in. Your first task as an investor is to decide what your primary goal is and, by extension, which of the three market types best meets your needs. The three types are cash flow markets, appreciation markets, and hybrid markets.

Appreciation markets are those that have high price appreciation but generally have either negative cash flow or low cash flow. Most of California falls into this category, as does Seattle, Boston, Manhattan, and other high-priced markets. These are good for investors with high-paying jobs and a longer time horizon who want to grow their net worth over time.

At the other end of the spectrum, cash flow markets give you the maximum cash-on-cash return (CCR) per invested dollar and are a good choice for someone nearing retirement who's looking to replace the income from a day job. However, these markets tend not to appreciate very much. An example of such a market would be Detroit, MI. You can buy a house there for $70,000 that rents for $800/month so it will cash flow very well, but 10 years from now that house will still be worth about $70,000 in today's dollars.

Hybrid markets offer a little of both: Some cash flow—though not as much as you'd get in a pure cash flow market—and some appreciation—but not as much as you'd get in an appreciation market. The major Florida and Texas metros offer appreciation but also a break-even or slightly better than break-even cash flow as well. These are good for investors who want to "hedge their bets" and get appreciation, yet can handle fluctuations in cash flow e.g., when there's a vacancy.

Here are some examples of well-known markets and where they fit in the scheme of things:

Exhibit 1.2: Matrix of Popular Real-Estate Markets

		Negative	Positive	High
APPRECIATION	High	Boston New York San Francisco Seattle		
	Medium		Atlanta Charlotte Houston Kansas City	
	Low			Birmingham Cincinnati Detroit Indianapolis

CASH FLOW

A word about risk and rewards: Over time, more of your returns will come from appreciation than from cash flow, but current cash flow is a safer bet than future appreciation.

Taking the hybrid market example above, if your Atlanta property nets $250/month, your cash returns after 10 years would be $3,000 per year x 10 years = $30,000 in today's dollars, assuming rents keep pace with inflation. But over that same 10-year period, that property might appreciate $100,000. So, of your total return of $130,000, 77% ($100,000) will come from the appreciation.

But as is always the case with investing, to get higher returns, you have to assume higher risk. The risk is that you invest in a property and it doesn't appreciate as you had hoped. Maybe interest rates go up and the market cools off, or maybe home builders over-build and put too many homes on the market at the same time and prices actually decline. Now you have a property that's not cash-flowing and not appreciating. In the long run, it will likely appreciate, but the wait can be vexing.

SOLVING FINANCIAL PROBLEMS WITH REAL ESTATE

Long-term wealth building

If you're a decade or two away from retirement e.g., in your forties, and you like your day job, you might want to invest for appreciation. That will grow your net worth the most and the fastest so that when you're ready to retire, you can sell each appreciated house and use the proceeds to buy multiple cash flow houses or a small multifamily to help replace the income from your day job.

Retirement

If you're nearing retirement, you don't have ten or twenty years to wait for appreciation to happen. You need cash flow now to replace the income from your day job. So you might want to invest for current cash flow in a stable market.

College fund

Some investors use real estate to fund their kids' college. Here's how it works: When your child is born, you buy an investment property in a hybrid market but on a 15-year, fully amortized loan. Even with a 15-year mortgage, the monthly rent can cover the expenses and by the time your kid is fifteen years old, you'll own the property free-and-clear—just in time for college! At that point, your $200,000 home might be worth $300,000 and you can sell it to pay for college expenses or keep it as a rental and use the cash flow to pay for your child's tuition and living expenses.

By buying one house for each child the year he or she is born, you can be well ahead of the game when it comes time to pay for their education.

Balanced portfolio

Finally, the decision to invest for appreciation vs. cash flow vs. both is not necessarily an either/or proposition. Many of my clients have one cash flow market and one appreciation market as part of a balanced portfolio. It's similar to having a diversified portfolio of stocks and bonds in your 401(k). Or you could invest in hybrid markets that offer a little cash flow and a little appreciation.

Before you go researching for markets and properties, you first have to decide what your goal is, and then determine which markets fit your criteria.

These are some of the factors that will determine your investment strategy.

In this book, we will be focusing on buy-and-hold investing (either through a turnkey provider or new construction) but it helps to be aware of other strategies as well.

CHAPTER 2
TURNKEY PROVIDERS

Now we'll discuss the concept of a turnkey provider, why you might want to buy your investment properties this way, and how you can pick the right one.

THE TURNKEY INVESTING MODEL

If you're like most investors, you'll find that the best market to invest in is not the market where you live. Oftentimes the market you're interested in is hundreds or thousands of miles from where you reside, and it's scary investing that far from home where you can't keep tabs on your investment.

Enter the turnkey provider!

A turnkey provider is a company that buys properties, renovates them, puts property management and tenants in place, and then offers them for sale to investors. It's the turnkey company's job to do the "heavy lifting" and assume most of the risk, thereby making it easier for remote investors like yourself to invest in their market.

How turnkey companies operate

Their first step in the process is to source the deal. This is done by examining a list of distressed properties available from bank foreclosure departments, auctions, or wholesalers.

To make the deal work, they have to make sure that the numbers make sense—i.e., that the acquisition cost plus repair cost plus holding costs allow sufficient margin for the deal to be profitable for them.

Therefore, for each property, they must first establish rent levels for the neighborhood. For example, "This is an $800/month neighborhood—that's what a tenant would be willing to pay to live here." They know this from their deep understanding of the market, verifiable by looking for rental "comps" in the same neighborhood. ("Comps" is short for "comparables" i.e., what have similar properties in the same neighborhood rented for recently?)

Once they know what the finished property would rent for, they have to determine the After-Repair Value (ARV) an investor would be willing to pay. This is often done by using the 1% rule: Most cash flow investors are looking to get 1% of the purchase price in monthly rent. For example, if a property is worth $100,000 and can rent for $1,000 a month, it will cash flow. In our example, the turnkey provider knows this property will rent for $800 a month, he can infer that an investor would be willing to pay about $80,000 for that property.

The next step is to inspect the property and determine a rehab budget, focusing on the five major systems first. The "Big Five" are: foundation, roof, electrical, plumbing, and HVAC. Once the major systems are renovated, any leftover budget can be used for cosmetics like kitchen countertops or bathroom tiles. But the important thing is to focus on the mechanicals so that the investor is unlikely to have any major repairs after acquiring the property.

Once the turnkey provider knows how much an investor would be willing to pay and how much it will cost them to renovate the property, he can back into his Maximum Allowable Price. This is shown in Exhibit 2.1:

Exhibit 2.1: Maximum Allowable Acquisition Price Calculation

After-Repair Value (ARV)	$80,000
- Renovation Costs	$30,000
- Profit Needed	$10,000
= Maximum Allowable Acquisition Price	$40,000

In this example, if an investor would pay $80,000 for the property and it's going to cost $30,000 to renovate it, and the turnkey provider needs to make $10,000 profit to make it worth his while, then the most the turnkey provider can afford to pay for the property is $40,000.

During the financial crisis of 2008-10, there were fore-closed homes everywhere and it was easy to find properties at a low-enough acquisition cost to have a viable turnkey business. Now that real estate markets have recovered nationwide, it's harder to make the numbers work at today's prices.

In any event, when you the investor purchase the property from the turnkey provider, you'll be getting it at or close to market price. After all, the turnkey provider could sell it to an owner-occupant on MLS at market price—why should he sell it for less to an investor?

How turnkey is turnkey?

In theory, the turnkey property should have no major problems and should generate cash flow for you on day one. The reality is that rehab quality varies from house to house. Some so-called turnkey providers will throw a coat of paint on the house and call it turnkey when they haven't really made much improvement to it. Some put their budget into cosmetics like nice fixtures, granite kitchen countertops, and tiles to make it sell quickly, but the mechanics of the house have not been upgraded. Properties like this will cost you money down the road, as your tenant discovers that major systems are in need of repair.

Beware of turnkey providers who focus on the cosmetics at the expense of the major systems! This is where your professional property inspection comes into play, which we will discuss in more detail later.

Major turnkey providers

There are dozens of turnkey providers around the country. Some operate only in one city, and these should be viewed with caution. If all they have to offer you is a house in Toledo, Ohio, then that's what they'll try to sell you—even if Toledo is not the best market for you. On the other hand, larger turnkey providers operate in multiple markets around the country, and thus can offer you a menu of options so you can pick the market that best suits your needs.

Exhibit 2.2 summarizes some of the top turnkey providers, what markets they offer, and what's unique about each of them.

Exhibit 2.2: Comparison of Multi-City Turnkey providers (2021)

Turnkey provider	Number of Markets	States	Comments
Jason Hartman JasonHartman.com	8	Florida, Tennessee, Pennsylvania, Ohio, Arkansas, Indiana, Mississippi, Missouri	Provides 10-year projected financial statements.
International Capital Group www.icgre.com	8	Florida, Georgia, Louisiana, North Carolina, Oklahoma	Works well with international (non-US) investors.
Norada Norada.com	27	Alabama, Arkansas, Florida, Georgia, Idaho, Indiana, Illinois, Iowa, Michigan, Missouri, Maryland, Ohio, Oklahoma, Tennessee, Texas, Utah, Wisconsin	Deal Grader property scoring system.
Real Wealth Network RealWealth.com	16	Alabama, Florida, Georgia, Illinois, Indiana, Maryland, Michigan, North Carolina, Ohio, Texas	Only provider that has a Six Sigma Black Belt* on staff to standardize processes and the quality control of the rehab and property management.

* An elite efficiency expert certification

Another advantage of working through a turnkey provider is that you have some protection. Even if you own only one house, you have much more clout with the property management company because you're part of a larger network that sends that property manager a lot of business. They're more likely to try to keep you happy than if you were investing by yourself.

For example, if the turnkey provider starts getting negative feedback from its customers about, say Toledo, then the turnkey provider will cut the Toledo provider off and not send any more investors until the problem is sorted out.

So, one of your first decisions to make is: Do I want to invest through a larger network of investors, or go solo? For beginning investors starting out with little experience, it's much safer to invest through a network! Buying a house on your own a thousand miles away is not only scary (meaning you may never "pull the trigger") but it's also much riskier.

CHAPTER 3
MARKETS

If you're working with a turnkey provider, they should have done the market research ahead of time and the markets they recommend should meet most of the criteria we're about to discuss. Nevertheless, as part of your due diligence you should do a reality check on the markets they offer.

If you're dealing with a provider who offers only one market—or if you're identifying markets on your own—then you'll want to follow the steps in this chapter rather rigorously.

That said, let's look at what makes a good market.

JOB GROWTH

The first thing I look for is job growth. With more jobs comes more workers and therefore more tenants.

Hospitals and universities tend to be more stable during economic downturns—and you *will* experience economic downturns over the time you own your property. So it's good to be thinking ahead about the number and stability of the jobs in the area.

New jobs also have a ripple effect through the local economy. For example, Toyota is currently building a factory in Huntsville, Alabama, that is expected to create 4,000 new jobs by 2021. Each of those auto workers will buy groceries, eat in restaurants, enroll kids in school, get cars repaired, etc., which creates more jobs in the process. It's not unusual for 4,000 primary jobs to create an equal number of secondary jobs in a local metro.

Where do you find this information? You can Google "<city name> chamber of commerce" and find the economic outlook and forecast on the city's Chamber of Commerce site. Or just Google <city name> and major employers.

If it's a large metro such as Atlanta, you may wind up investing in the suburbs or surrounding towns. You'll want to keep an eye on what jobs are within commuting distance of whatever property you're considering. Some surrounding cities have local job centers in addition to being commutable to the larger city.

If your property is in a surrounding city that has fewer local jobs of its own, or is a "bedroom community" suburb of a major city, you could get hit with more vacancies whenever there's a recession.

STABILITY

Another characteristic of a good investment market is stability. You don't want a market that booms in good times and crashes in bad times. Below we'll discuss some factors that help make a market stable:

- Diverse economy

- Workforce stability

- Population growth

- Demographics

- Infrastructure

- Inventory – Supply and Demand

Diverse economy

A local economy with many employers in varied industries is more stable, because if one segment of the economy is doing poorly, employment in other segments of the economy can pick up the slack.

You can find this out by Googling <city name> and "top employers." You should wind up with something that looks like this table for Atlanta:

Exhibit 3.1: List of Top Atlanta Employers

Employer	Number of employees
Delta Air Lines	31,237
Emory University / Emory Healthcare	29,937
Wal-Mart Stores, Inc.	20,532
The Home Depot	20,000
AT&T	17,882
The Kroger Co.	14,753
Wellstar Health Systems	24,000
Publix Super Markets, Inc.	9,494
USPS - Atlanta District	9,385
Northside Hospital	9,016
Coca-Cola	8,761
United Parcel Service	8,727
Piedmont Healthcare	8,707
Centers for Disease Control and Prevention	8,539
Children's Healthcare of Atlanta	7,452
Cox Enterprises Inc	7,255
Bank of America, N.A.	6,800
SunTrust Banks	6,800
Georgia Tech	6,386
Southern Company	6,247
Georgia State University	5,875

Source: Wikipedia

Notice how diverse the Atlanta economy is! Coca Cola, SunTrust Bank, Delta Airlines, Home Depot, UPS, the Center for Disease Control are all headquartered there. Not to mention all the healthcare companies, universities, and Hartfield Airport—the busiest airport in the world.

For example, as of this writing, Delta Airlines is suffering because of the Covid-19 virus, but Amazon is hiring and the Center for Disease Control is expanding. Contrast this with Detroit—which despite that city's efforts to diversify its economy—is still heavily dependent on the "Big Three" auto companies and their suppliers:

Exhibit 3.2: List of Top Employers in Detroit

Rank	Company	City	Detroit Region Employment
1	Ford Motor Co.	Dearborn	48,000
2	General Motors Co.	Detroit	37,400
3	FCA US LLC	Auburn Hills	35,399
4	University of Michigan	Ann Arbor	34,067
5	Beaumont Health	Southfield	28,012
6	Henry Ford Health System	Detroit	23,724
7	U.S. government	Detroit	18,817
8	Rock Ventures	Detroit	17,819
9	Trinity Health	Livonia	15,899
10	Ascension Michigan	Warren	11,893
11	U.S. Postal Service	Detroit	11,805
12	Detroit Medical Center	Detroit	10,047
13	City of Detroit	Detroit	9,565
14	State of Michigan	Detroit	9,458
15	Blue Cross Blue Shield of MI/Blue care Network	Detroit	7,266
16	DTE Energy Co.	Detroit	6,740
17	Illitch Companies	Detroit	6,740
18	Wayne State University	Detroit	5,910
19	Detroit Public Schools Community District	Detroit	5,700
20	McLaren Health Care Corp	Grand Blanc	5,551
21	Magna International of America Inc.	Troy	5,095
22	Comerica Bank	Detroit	4,486

Source: DetroitChamber.com

Note that the top three employers are auto companies employing over 120,000 directly – and many more indirectly.

To make matters worse, as of this writing the auto industry is going through disruption, with new technologies emerging for electric, hybrid, and self-driving cars, to say nothing of eliminating car ownership altogether through ride-sharing services. Who knows how all that is going to play out? Ten years from now, the auto industry landscape may look very different from what it looks like today.

The next time the auto industry has a downturn (like the one in 2009) or the next time there's a recession, Detroit could get hit harder than most metros. A diverse economy with multiple industries is the safest way to go when it comes to single-family home investing.

Extra for Experts

In larger metros like Atlanta, you might want to drill down and look at micro-markets (or sub-markets), as some sections of the city or suburbs are growing faster than others.

For example, the Atlanta airport is located on the southwest side of the city. Let's say you own properties in that area and due to a global pandemic, the airline industry goes into a slump. It won't matter that much that Atlanta's economy is diversified overall; what will matter is how diversified the economy is within commuting distance of your property. Atlanta overall may be thriving, but your little corner of Atlanta may not be.

On a map, plot the location of major employers within driving distance of the property you're considering, and make sure that local economy is diversified as well.

Workforce stability

In addition to a diverse economy, you should also consider the stability of the jobs in the metro.

In the Detroit example, your strategy could be to rent to tenants in industries like healthcare: nurses, ambulance drivers, EMTs, X-ray technicians, and health insurance personnel all make good tenants as they are in a stable industry that doesn't have the ups-and-downs of the auto industry. Government jobs (especially federal) tend to be very reliable. During the Covid-19 pandemic, over twenty million Americans lost their jobs. How many federal government bureaucrats lost their jobs? Very few or none.

Another example is retirees. There are many communities in Florida with large retirement populations, and they're not sensitive to economic cycles at all. Retirees don't need jobs; in fact, retirees actually attract jobs: For every thousand retirees, a metro area will need more healthcare providers, restaurant workers, and grounds keepers for the golf courses, and those jobs are largely stable.

If you're considering a market with a less-diverse economy, the next best thing is to find the most stable tenants within that economy.

Population growth

This is something you should get right, as population growth can solve a lot of your investment concerns. If the population is growing, then the demand for housing will grow, which means your rents and property values are likely to grow. Vacancies become less problematic in a market where the population is growing.

I track population growth separately from job growth, because some areas of the country—such as Florida—have population growth driven by retirees, and while retirees do bring jobs, they don't bring as many as would an equivalent number of working-aged people. As a result, the rate of population growth can be greater than the rate of job growth.

Sources of population growth information

Census.gov – The Census Bureau keeps track of population trends nationwide.

Trucking companies – Trucking companies like U-Haul also provide good insights into where populations are increasing and decreasing. For example, I went to the U-Haul site and got quotes for two truck rentals:

- San Francisco to Denver: $2,447

- Denver to San Francisco: $914

The distances for each quote are the same; why does one cost almost three times as much as the other? The reason is there are so many more people leaving San Francisco than entering (decline in population) that when the truck is driven to Denver, U-Haul has to pay someone to drive it back to San Francisco. That is a clue. Just Google "U-Haul Press Releases Migration Trends" to get the latest stats on where people are moving to and from.

Extra for Experts: Segmenting the Population

Another way to refine population trends is to look at population by socio-economic status:

- Wealthy
- Affluent
- White collar
- Blue collar
- Unskilled labor
- Unemployed/Homeless

The "sweet spot" for most real estate investors is workforce tenants: the school teacher, the nurse, the ambulance driver, the cop, or the auto parts store manager. What's most important to you, the investor, is not that a metro area's population is growing *overall*, it's whether the population of *prospective tenants* is growing.

For example, Cleveland's overall population *decreased* by -1.0% in 2018, but the Cleveland Clinic (hospital chain) is expanding and the population of nurses, X-ray technicians, paramedics, EMTs, and other medical professionals—i.e., the population of good tenants—is increasing.

As of this writing, there are 75,000 unfilled medical jobs open in Cleveland. Most of them could be your tenants.

As an investor, do you care how many millionaires or how many homeless people enter or leave Cleveland each year? Maybe a little, but those people aren't going to be your tenants. What matters most to you is whether your target tenant's population is growing.

Go to any of the major job sites and do a search for jobs in or around the zip code of the property you're considering, and get a sense of how the population of tenants (not the overall population) is growing in that area (not the city as a whole).

Demographics

Related to population growth is demographics of that growth, such as education level and household income. These are critical pieces of information for determining where to invest and who your target renter is likely to be.

Numerous websites offer such information, but two that I like in particular are: www.City-Data.com and www. Niche.com.

Using Huntsville, AL, as an example, City-Data.com gives us this snapshot of the area's demographics:

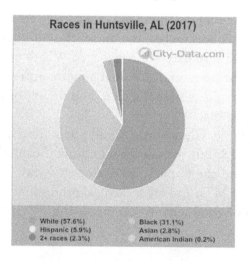

Population in 2017: 194,585 (97% urban, 3% rural).
Population change since 2000: +23.0%

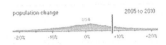

Males: 92,327 (47.4%)
Females: 102,258 (52.6%)

Median resident age: 37.3 years
Alabama median age: 38.9 years

Zip codes: 35649, 35741, 35757, 35758, 35759, 35763, 35801, 35802, 35803, 35805,

Huntsville Zip Code Map

Estimated median household income in 2017: $50,704 (it was $41,074 in 2000)
Huntsville: $50,704
AL: $48,123

Estimated per capita income in 2017: $33,656 (it was $24,015 in 2000)

Huntsville city income, earnings, and wages data

Estimated median house or condo value in 2017: $170,900 (it was $95,600 in 2000)
Huntsville: $170,900
AL: $141,300

This information can help you get a feel for the area and the type of people you may be renting to—before you spend money on a plane ticket to investigate in person.

Niche.com provides additional information about Huntsville:

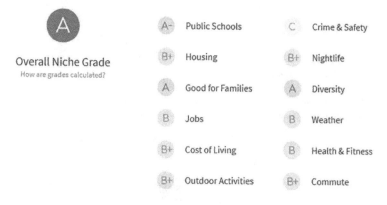

A- Public Schools	C Crime & Safety
B+ Housing	B+ Nightlife
A Good for Families	A Diversity
B Jobs	B Weather
B+ Cost of Living	B Health & Fitness
B+ Outdoor Activities	B+ Commute

Overall Niche Grade
How are grades calculated?

Real Estate

Median Home Value
$176,100
National $184,700

Median Rent
$804
National $949

Area Feel @
Dense Suburban

Rent vs. Own

Rent	42%
Own	58%

Residents

Diversity

 A Based on ethnic and economic diversity.

Age

<10 years	12%
10-17 years	9%
18-24 years	11%

Education Levels National

Master's degree or higher	17%	12%
Bachelor's degree	26%	19%
Some college or associate's degree	28%	29%

Infrastructure

Another characteristic of a good market is growth in infrastructure, such as new highways, shopping centers, and expanded airports. These investments are made because public officials or captains of industry have done their homework and concluded that these investments are worthwhile.

For example, if the population of an area is projected to grow, funds will be earmarked to build new freeways and roads, and to expand utility services like water and power. The city planners have done a lot more research than you or I ever will, so when you discover funding has been approved for certain projects, that's validation that the area you're investing in is growing and is poised for even more growth.

How do you find this information? You can look at the city's Chamber of Commerce website, economic development website, or just Google it. Here's what a Google search of "Orlando new freeways" produced:

https://www.orlandoedc.com/Locate-Expand/
Infrastructure/Transportation/Roads.aspx
https://www.bisnow.com/south-florida/news/
construction-development/florida-new-highways-98515

If you don't see any future infrastructure projects in the pipeline, you have to ask yourself why that is and whether this is an area you want to invest in.

Inventory – Supply and Demand

Some markets suffer at times from overbuilding, such as Miami or San Diego during the 2008 global financial crisis, resulting in a glut of housing on the market at the same time and a drop in prices. As an investor, you'll want to protect yourself from this outcome.

Here's what happens: An area exhibits job and population growth, and real estate developers take notice. If the growth looks like it'll last, then developers will start the process of buying land, applying for building permits, hiring workers to bulldoze the land, build lots, and eventually construct houses.

The problem is that process takes years. In some municipalities (e.g., all of California) just getting the permits alone can take years, let alone the time it takes to line up construction financing and actually start building. By the time the houses come on the market, the economy might have turned, and the builders have to radically drop prices. That $150,000 house you thought was going to appreciate to $200,000 is now worth only $130,000, and you're "underwater" with your mortgage.

To protect yourself against this, you should Google the City Planning Commission website for the metro you're considering. Note how many housing permits have been approved and are in the pipeline and see what you can learn.

Another resource is www.NewHomeSource.com, which is a directory of all new housing developments in the US. Looking again at Huntsville, AL, we see that there are seventy-five new communities being built, and most of the homes are in the $225K - $400K range. Your $150,000 rental is unlikely to be affected by this new inventory. If anything, having such higher-priced homes in your neighborhood might improve your property values.

Exhibit 3.3: Screenshot of NewHomeSource.com

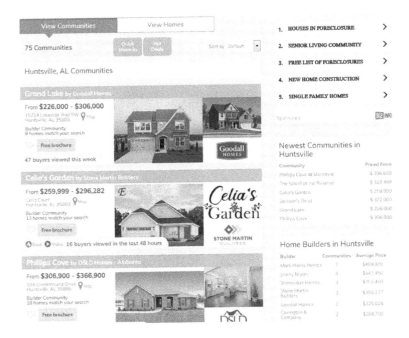

MARKET SIZE

Another factor to consider is the size of the metro you plan to invest in. Most real estate investors flock to the major metros like Charlotte, Atlanta, Nashville, etc. What about secondary or tertiary markets that aren't already saturated with investors?

That approach can work, but there are several caveats. Let's take an extreme example of a city with a population of 20,000, like Elko, NV. The town is experiencing a boom of sorts, as there's lots of mining and natural gas exploration there, and it's certainly not on the radar of most investors. Here are some considerations with small towns like Elko:

More risk

A small city is not as resilient as a major metro. If one major employer in a small town shuts down, the entire local economy will feel the effects. If one home builder builds too many homes and puts them on the market at the same time, housing prices will collapse. A major metro like Dallas could absorb those developments without batting an eye. But in a small metro, changes can have large—and long-lasting—impacts. Similarly, you'll have more risk with your exit strategy. When you go to sell your property, the pool of available buyers is much smaller in a small metro than in a major metro.

Property management

Even in major metros, it's hard to find good property management companies that are capable, efficient, and honest. I personally won't invest in a market unless I've identified two good property managers, so if the first one doesn't work out for any reason, I have a backup property manager already identified. In a small metro, you'd be lucky to find one—let alone two—good property management companies. What if the one you've chosen doesn't work out?

How I'd play it

I would invest in a small metro only if it is within driving distance of a major metro and, even better, if it's in the "path of progress" of the local major metro. An example is Greenville, TX, (pop 28,000), about thirty miles east of Dallas.

Businesses had been finding Dallas too expensive and congested and had been expanding their operations further away from Dallas, but still close to it. Accelerating this trend is the Covid-19 pandemic, which made companies realize that the remote-employee model actually works! They don't need to pay higher salaries to recruit employees in the major metros.

So small metros like Greenville, TX, are remote enough for tenants to enjoy the benefits of remote living, but still close enough to a major metro that they can commute if the local employer shuts down, plus they can easily access sporting events or other big-city amenities. And as more-and-more companies move further away from Dallas, Greenville will become more developed and property values should go up.

But aside from small metros near major metros being in the path of progress, I'd stick to metros that have populations of 500,000 or more with diverse economies.

LANDLORD-TENANT LAWS

Another characteristic of a good market is one in which landlord-tenant laws favor the landlord or, at the very least, are neutral.

Some states like California, New York, or Massachusetts have very tenant-biased laws, where it could take six months to evict a tenant who hasn't been paying rent. In other cases, you have to look at the policies of individual cities within a state.

For example, in Chicago there's a city ordinance that forbids evicting someone if the temperature is below zero. That is done for humanitarian reasons—you don't want to throw someone out on the street in the dead of winter—but a street-smart tenant who knows how to game the system could stop paying rent in November and you won't be able to evict him until March. In the meantime, you're losing money.

In other states like Arkansas, Texas, and Arizona, a non-paying tenant can be evicted in a matter of weeks, with a sheriff's deputy showing up and escorting them off the premises.

How to find out how the local laws work? Ask your property manager: What's the process for eviction? How long does it take on average to evict a tenant?

Attend local Real Estate Investor Associations (REIAs) or investing meetup groups, which are a great resource for getting the lay of the land in a given market. You can network with other investors and get the inside scoop on eviction laws and other issues related to a market.

Rule of thumb: Not to get political, but in general, your conservative "red" states like Texas and Florida are more landlord-friendly, and your liberal "blue" states like California or New York are more tenant-friendly. But consult with your property manager to confirm the local practices.

NATURAL DISASTERS

Another factor in your choice of markets is how much weight to place on natural disasters such as the hurricanes that impact Florida and other Gulf Coast states.

Weather happens. Gulf states have hurricanes. The Midwest has tornadoes and hailstorms. California has earthquakes and wildfires (not really weather, but still natural disasters). As an investor, you can avoid these areas, but know that a *lot* of money has been made investing in real estate in these areas.

The first way to manage this risk is obviously through insurance. Get quotes for insurance policies that cover not only damage to the property but also lost rents while the property is being repaired. Your mortgage payment will be due whether the tenant still lives there or has moved out until the water and roof damage is repaired. Factor the added insurance coverage into your property pro forma and, if the investment still makes financial sense, move forward.

A second way to manage this risk is by choosing certain areas of a metro to invest in and avoiding other areas. For example, Houston is a growing metro on the Gulf Coast, with great job and population growth. If you look at a map of Houston, you'll see that there's an east-west freeway called I-10 that cuts the city in half:

Exhibit 3.4: Map of Houston

Source: Google Maps

A lot of growth in the Houston metro is northward, toward The Woodlands and further. If you purchase property north of I-10, the hurricane risk is a lot less than if you purchase property south of I-10.

To find this out, pick a metro south of I-10 (like Baytown, TX) and a metro north of I-10 (like Spring, TX) and ask your insurance company to provide quotes for a four-bedroom, two-bath, 1,800-square foot house in each area. If you find the insurance quote for hurricane and flooding is much higher in certain parts of the Houston metro than others, then you know there's more hurricane risk there.

Personally, if I were investing in Houston, I'd stay north of I-10.

WHAT ABOUT CLIMATE CHANGE?

Whether you believe in climate change or not, the people you sell your property to someday may, and so it's important to consider how the property you're considering purchasing is affected by climate change. If you buy beachfront property in Florida—will it be under water in ten years? Will enough people be concerned that it will be under water that you'll have trouble selling it?

To answer these questions, you can go to the National Oceanic and Atmospheric Administration (NOAA) "Sea Level Rise Viewer" site to get an objective scientific assessment. Here's the direct link: https://coast.noaa.gov/digitalcoast/tools/slr.html.

Here's a screenshot of that site showing what would happen to San Francisco if sea levels were to rise six feet. (The sliding scale on the left enables you to dial the sea level up or down as you wish.)

As you can see, San Francisco, hilly as it is, isn't much affected by sea levels rising six feet, but the San Francisco Airport (the lighter area at the bottom-right of the screenshot below) would be completely under water.

Exhibit 3.5: Screenshot of San Francisco Sea Levels

Now, how likely is it that sea levels will rise six feet? For that, you click on the "Local Scenario" button in the left-hand menu, and you'll get NOAA's best guess as to how likely that scenario is. In the screenshot below, we can see that sea levels aren't expected to rise 5.71 feet until the year 2100, so someone investing in San Francisco in 2020 is probably ok.

Exhibit 3.6: Screenshot of San Francisco Local Scenario

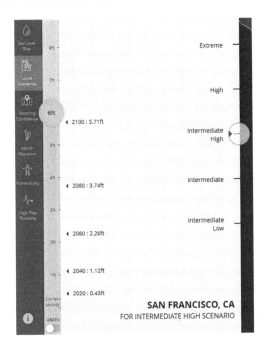

As you can see, sea levels around San Francisco won't approach six feet until the year 2100, so if you buy a property there today, you have little to worry about. Anytime you're investing in a coastal area and are concerned about the effects of climate change on your investment, this tool can help you make your decision.

MARKET CYCLES AND TIMING

All real estate is local. At any given time, some markets in the United States are just starting to take off, others are expanding, others are peaking, and others are in decline. Before making an investment as major as real estate, you should know where your market is in its cycle.

Exception

One exception to this was the Global Financial Crisis of 2008-10, in which most, if not all, US markets were in distress at the same time. This was because the root of the crisis was systemic problems with the entire US banking system. That should be a once-in-a-lifetime event and, now that we're back to normal, local real estate markets should perform more-or-less independently of each other based on what's going on in local economies.

The diagram and captions below illustrate how real estate cycles work:

Exhibit 3.7: Real Estate Cycles

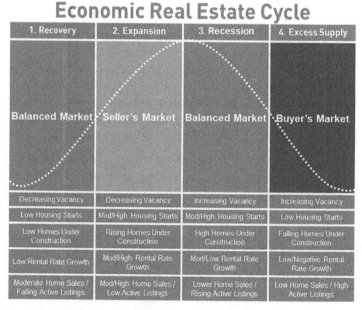

Economic Real Estate Cycle

1. Recovery	2. Expansion	3. Recession	4. Excess Supply
Balanced Market	Seller's Market	Balanced Market	Buyer's Market
Decreasing Vacancy	Decreasing Vacancy	Increasing Vacancy	Increasing Vacancy
Low Housing Starts	Mod/High Housing Starts	Mod/High Housing Starts	Low Housing Starts
Low Homes Under Construction	Rising Homes Under Construction	High Homes Under Construction	Falling Homes Under Construction
Low Rental Rate Growth	Mod/High Rental Rate Growth	Mod/Low Rental Rate Growth	Low/Negative Rental Rate Growth
Moderate Home Sales / Falling Active Listings	Mod/High Home Sales / Low Active Listings	Lower Home Sales / Rising Active Listings	Low Home Sales / High Active Listings

Source: Mortgage Sandbox

Examples

An example of this cycle would be Huntsville AL.

Huntsville was for many years a stable, balanced market but today it's definitely in the Expansion phase. Toyota is opening a factory there in 2021 that will create 4,000 new jobs, and the FBI is moving over 2,000 jobs from Virginia to Huntsville.

New home builders are building new developments all over town, investors are having a hard time finding properties to buy, and available rentals are getting multiple tenant applications. I would guess that Huntsville is in the second inning of what will be a 10-15 year expansion cycle.

After this expansion, the market will likely stabilize and, if home builders don't time it right, there might be an oversupply of homes hitting the market after job growth tapers off.

Also note that the "Recovery" phase shown in the graph is not inevitable. Some markets may never recover if the jobs and population continue to drop.

LOCAL MARKET CONSIDERATIONS

A local realtor with decades of experience would have an intuitive grasp of her local market, so you should consult her, but you should take what she says with a grain of salt. Realtors always say, "Now is the perfect time to buy!" no matter what the conditions. It therefore behooves you to independently confirm what information she's giving you. You do that by looking at local market indicators. Sites like Realtor.com, Trulia.com, Zillow.com, and Redfin.com are great sources of information.

Days on market

Days on Market (DOM) is a measure of how many calendar days a property is on the market before someone buys it. In a hot market, a property may sell within hours and in a dead market, a property could languish for a year or more. If DOM is consistently increasing month-after-month, that's a sign the market has peaked and is slowing down. Conversely, if DOM is shortening, then demand is outpacing supply and properties are being snapped up quickly.

Multiple offers

Related to DOM is multiple offers. In a hot market, a property available for sale might receive multiple offers, some over the asking price. In San Jose in 2018, a house listed for $1,000,000 might receive a dozen offers within days and finally sell for 20% above the asking price.

Months of inventory

Months of Inventory is another measure of how "hot" the local market is. It's calculated by taking the total number of homes available for sale at a given time and dividing that by the average number of properties sold per month. For example, if a metro area has 1,000 homes for sale and typically 250 homes sell each month, then that metro has four months of inventory.

A normal, equilibrium market has about six months of inventory at any given time. If there are fewer than that, say only three months of inventory, then it's a seller's market because there's more demand than supply. However, if there are nine months of inventory, that means there's too much supply, prices will likely be soft, so it's a good time to be a buyer.

Extra for Experts: New Residential Permits

Another local indicator is how much new home construction is in the pipeline. This information can be obtained by looking through any City Planning Commission website to find information on new residential housing permits, by year.

In most metros, the number of new homes entering the market doesn't skew prices for the market that much, but the fact that builders are applying for permits and cities are granting them is a bullish sign that the local real estate market is in a healthy phase.

Price trends

Zillow's "Home Value Index" gives a good indication of where a market is in its cycle. By typing in various cities in the "Compare" button on the bottom-right of the screen, you can easily compare the price trends of a three-bedroom house in each of the four major Alabama metros. Clearly, Tuscaloosa and Huntsville (top two lines) are on the upswing.

To access this, just Google "Zillow Home Value Index" or visit https://www.zillow.com/home-values/.

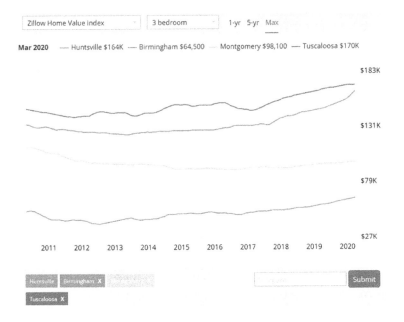

No matter where your market is in the market cycle, keep in mind that real estate is a long-term investment, and you may experience a down market at some point during the time you own the property.

Non-Local Market Considerations

So far, we've discussed factors specific to a given market to determine whether it's a good market in which to invest. The investor should be aware that there are also national and global factors that play into the desirability of local real estate markets.

Inflation

Monetary inflation is a nationwide occurrence driven by the rate at which the government prints money, as is done to help mitigate the effects of the Covid-19 crisis. This is separate from local inflation specific to markets such as the cost of land, cost of permits, supply and demand of labor and materials, etc.

Monetary inflation is created at the national level and can benefit real estate investors nationwide, as they get to pay off their mortgages in inflated dollars, and see their rents and property values rise, at least in nominal terms.

Interest Rates

Interest rates are also driven at the national level, influenced by how tight or loose the Federal Reserve is, or what the global demand is for 10-year US Treasury Notes.

Funds Flows

Funds flows can be national or international. If Nashville is perceived to be the "next hot market," then investors from all over the country will flow to that market. In some metros like San Francisco and Vancouver, BC, lots of money from

China is driving property prices up out of proportion to what local household incomes could justify. Hawaii real estate is often skewed by Japanese investors, as New York and Florida markets are often skewed by European investors.

To keep abreast of these factors, you should monitor the financial press, such as CNBC, CNBC.com, Barron's, the Wall Street Journal, and other sources. To keep an eye on the foreign money, pay special attention to foreign exchange rates. If the Australian dollar gets strong relative to the US dollar, then US real estate will become very cheap to Australians and you can expect funds to flow from Australia to the US.

Also, investors from different countries have different preferences for markets. Europeans seem to think of the United States in terms of only two states: New York and Florida. South American investors like Miami. Japanese investors like Hawaii, and Chinese investors like California and Vancouver, BC. Of course, these are generalizations, but they can help you focus on which markets are likely to benefit from exchange rate fluctuations.

You don't need to turn this into a full-time job by reading the financial press every day. Just check in periodically so you know what's going on in the world beyond your chosen market.

HOW MANY MARKETS SHOULD YOU INVEST IN?

No discussion of markets would be complete without addressing how many markets an investor should invest in. There's a tradeoff between diversification on the one hand and focus on the other.

Let's take an extreme case and suppose you own ten properties in ten different states. What would that be like?

For every state where you own income property, you'll have to file income tax returns in that state. Your returns could be 120 pages every year. (Exceptions: Seven states don't have a state income tax: Alaska, Florida, Nevada, South Dakota, Texas, Washington and Wyoming.)

You'll be dealing with ten different property management companies, possibly ten different reporting systems, and you would be a small client for each of them.

You wouldn't acquire a deep understanding of any of the markets—their neighborhoods, job centers, or traffic patterns because you're too spread out and can't focus on any one market.

You would have a hard time keeping tabs on your investments because the cost of flying out to see your properties (airfare, hotel, rental car) would eat up your cash flow for the year.

At the other extreme, suppose you own all ten properties in one market and property values plummet due to overbuilding (San Diego 2006), or major employers declare bankruptcy (Detroit 2009), or rent control is implemented (San Francisco 2020)? By having all your eggs in one basket, you've painted yourself into a corner and lack diversification.

I recommend a balanced approach in which you have a critical mass of properties in several areas, so you have both diversification and focus. What constitutes a "critical mass?"

In the above example, I think you could prudently own five houses in each of two markets to be diversified and still have deep knowledge of your markets. You will also know the property management teams well; they will be more responsive to your needs, since you're a relatively "major" client to both property management companies with five houses in each (vs. being a small client to ten different property management companies). It would also be cost-effective for you to fly out to visit your properties every so often, given that you have a critical mass in each area.

Alternatively, you could own three or four properties in three different markets. This works especially well when the markets are close to each other. For example, if you owned properties across various markets in Alabama—e.g., Montgomery, Birmingham, Huntsville, and Tuscaloosa, with different economies and within an hour's drive of Birmingham in the center of the state—you could enjoy geographic and economic diversification all in one area, and only file one income tax return each year.

Other examples of markets within driving distance of each other include Cincinnati and Indianapolis, Columbus and Cleveland, Orlando and Tampa, Memphis and Nashville.

SURF BEFORE YOU FLY

When considering a place to invest, it is most cost-effective to do as much research as you can online ("web-surfing") rather than incurring travel expenses by going in-person. It's really discouraging to plan a trip, fly out to a potential investment market, and find out in the first five minutes it's not going to work. (Ask me how I know.)

If you can do 90% of your research online, you can weed out areas that don't fit your criteria and then you can focus on a "short list" of promising markets and sub-markets. Only after you've done your research and have your short list of markets is it time to head to the airport. On the other hand, some investors ask me if they need to visit the market at all. Can't they just research online and buy sight unseen? In my opinion, you can do that, but you're taking more risk.

I've recently visited a new construction property near Atlanta and found it was located at the end of the street right near a big power line. I've had an investor buy a house that looked good online but found later that it was on a noisy street with lots of traffic, and therefore she had problems getting a tenant.

There's only so much you can do from your desktop. Nothing replaces going there in person, seeing the neighborhood, visiting the property, getting a "feel" for the area, meeting the leasing agents, and achieving a comfort level with your investment.

At the very least, I recommend you go out to visit the area and the property the first time. If you get a good comfort level with the area and with the integrity of the team you're working with (i.e., they've got your back) then you can make subsequent investments sight unseen.

Even if you're buying without having visited in person, I'd recommend you have the property manager's leasing agent provide you with a "virtual tour," whereby she walks through the house with a video camera room-by-room and points out the features of the home. I tell them to imagine that a prospective buyer or tenant is standing right next to them: How would you "sell" this property to a tenant?

So it's not a quick walkthrough, but a detailed inspection of the house: Point out the bathroom fixtures and tiles; the kitchen counters, backsplashes, and appliances; the overhead ceiling fans, the neutral paint colors and trim; the large, enclosed yard for kids' safe play; the new water heater and HVAC system, and so on. Particular emphasis should be placed on the kitchen and the master bath, as those are usually what "sells" a house.

Ideally, the virtual tour will include a view of the neighborhood. The leasing agent should slowly pan the camera up-and-down the street so you can see what it looks like. Do the neighbors mow their lawns and show pride of ownership? Are there nice cars visible, or clunkers? Any power lines near the property? Is it on a wide street with lots of noisy traffic, or a quiet cul-de-sac? In urban areas, is there a bus stop nearby where people may congregate and perhaps smoke cigarettes while they wait for the bus?

Finally, you should see if the leasing agent is willing to video the property behind the house (she will of course want to be discreet in doing so). Are there dogs barking? A couple yelling at each other? Is the fence on the common property line in disrepair?

In this Covid-19 era, many investors are reluctant to fly to visit the property in-person, so a virtual tour may be your best option. Just make sure it's detailed enough to answer most of your questions about the property and neighborhood. Tell the leasing agent in advance what you need to see in order to be comfortable buying a property.

As you can see from this chapter, doing an in-depth market analysis can be a lot of work. Not only do you have to become your own economist, but you might have to research five markets for every one you decide to invest in.

It's far easier to work with a turnkey provider who's already done the market research and ask them to share why they think a particular market is good for your investments. That said, it's still important for you, as the investor, to fact-check what others are telling you (and fill in any gaps in the information provided), and to independently arrive at your own conclusions. If you're a do-it-yourself investor, then this chapter is essential for you.

CHAPTER 4
PROPERTY MANAGEMENT

Property management is the number one reason investors fail.

As soon as you've found a market that looks promising, your next step is to identify at least one—preferably two—good property management companies. Why two? As noted previously, if your first property manager doesn't work out, you'll have a backup.

If you can't identify two good property management companies in a given market, you should think twice about investing there. Don't invest the time researching neighborhoods, properties, or financial projections until you've identified qualified, reliable property managers first, or you'll be wasting your time.

This is a reason why investors gravitate toward major metros. While it's tempting to invest in tertiary markets like Tyler, TX, or Altoona, PA, that aren't saturated with investors, it's really difficult to find one, let alone two, good property management companies in such markets.

I would rather own property in a mediocre market with a stellar property manager than own property in a stellar market with a mediocre property manager. The property manager can make or break your investment.

If you're investing through a turnkey provider, all this vetting of property management companies has already been done for you, so you may want to go with whomever the turnkey provider recommends.

This also offers you protection, since being part of a larger network gives you some clout with the property management company: The property manager will want to keep you happy because you're part of a network that sends the property manager a lot of business.

Even if you plan to use the property manager your turnkey provider recommends, you should still follow the steps in this chapter and the checklist at the end so you know what you're getting into and will have fewer surprises. You should evaluate a property manager the same way you screen tenants.

INTEGRITY

When evaluating any property management company, the first thing you want to know is: Are these people crooks?

War Story

I knew of one property manager in Kansas City (no longer in business); over the phone, she was just what you'd want: good knowledge of the market, lots of experience, good systems in place for screening tenants, and lots of street smarts. But she came down with a form of cancer that wasn't covered by her health insurance, so when she rented out homes, she didn't tell her out-of-state landlords that the places had been rented, and she pocketed the cash. Even a good person can make bad decisions when her back is up against the wall. The last I heard, the FBI was looking for her.

Be aware that some property managers use maintenance operation as a profit center, sending out a handyman for every little tenant service call. There are even crooked property managers who will claim they had to send a guy out to fix something that didn't need fixing, thus charging you for work that wasn't even done.

Some property managers will mark up service calls or send exorbitant invoices. This is not trivial. I had a client who needed a make-ready after her tenant vacated the property. She was quoted $2,100 by the property manager to remove trash, clean the carpets, and touch up some paint. So she hired someone herself to do the work—for $700!

How can you find out if your property manager is capable? The National Association of Residential Property Managers (www.Narpm.org) or NARPM (pronounced "NAR-pum") is *the* professional association for residential property managers. As part of your due diligence process, check to see if your property manager is a member, or even better, is the holder of one or more NARPM professional certifications. If your property manager is NOT associated with NARPM, that's not necessarily a deal-breaker, but it's reassuring to know if she is a member of the top industry association and has formal training in property management and professional ethics.

You can also check the Better Business Bureau (www. BBB.org) for *landlord* complaints to see if any of the issues above are mentioned. I would not place much stock in *tenant* complaints, as all property managers get those. "That property manager made me pay rent on time, and when I didn't, she evicted me!"

Other investors are probably your best source of information. In whatever market you're in, find the local Real Estate Investor Association (REIA) or go to Meetup.com and type "Real Estate Investing" and the zip code to find local clubs. By attending those, you can meet fellow investors and get the inside scoop on who has a good or bad reputation in a given market. A national directory of real estate investor clubs can be found here: https://members.reiclub.com/real-estate-clubs/.

Yelp.com will have reviews on your property management company, but keep in mind that most of them will be from tenants and therefore unfavorable. Happy tenants rarely report their experiences. Since you're the landlord, what you're really looking for is how happy *landlords* are with their property management company. You can check Yelp.com just to see if there are any insights to be gained, or any patterns like consistently bad reviews on handling repairs, but in general, the sources above will give you better insights.

Be cautious of real estate agents who manage properties on-the-side. In some real estate brokerages, there's an in-house property manager who helps investors with their properties. In many cases, this person was chosen because she was the lowest performer in the office. Think about it: If you're a real estate broker with ten agents working for you, who are you going to assign property management tasks to, your top seller? No! You want your top seller out there selling, making you money. What you'll do is take your poorest performer and give her an "opportunity to make extra cash while she's getting her sales up." Who knows? Maybe she's actually good at it; she found her niche and enjoys the role better than selling. I know a few stellar property managers who started that way. Just be aware.

Finally, it's preferable if your property management company has in-house leasing agents. If they use outside agents to find tenants, they may be less rigorous about finding *good* tenants because they won't have to deal with the tenants after they're placed.

FEE STRUCTURE

The next thing to check is the property manager's fee structure. Some have low monthly management fees, but then gouge you on other fees such as markups on maintenance, or tenant placement fees. It's best to create a table comparing all fees side-by-side, an example of which I'll provide at the end of this section.

Monthly management fee

The monthly management fee is usually 8-10% of collected rents, so for a $1,000 monthly rental, you'll pay $80 or $100 per month for property management. It may be lower for a new-construction home, as they are still under builder warranty and require less management.

Maintenance fees

Another source of fees is maintenance, such as sending out a handyman to unplug a toilet or replace a cracked window. It's generally better if the property manager has in-house handymen they can send out for routine repairs, as it is not only cheaper but also quicker since they control the handyman's time. An outside repair person might not be available right away.

At the opposite end of the spectrum is to have no work crews in-house and completely outsource this function with third-party vendors. This tends to be more expensive than in-house, especially when the property manager charges a markup of 10-15%. So, when a plumber charges $100 for a job, the property manager will charge you $115 because she had to schedule the plumber, then drive out to the property to let the plumber in.

A happy medium is when the property manager has in-housework crews for most repairs and some third-party crews for specialty work (like electrical) or overflow work during peak periods (e.g., air conditioning techs during the summer).

What the property manager should have is a list of third-party vendors by type (plumbers, electricians, HVAC, roofers, etc.) ranked by hourly rate. So when they need to call out a landscaper, for example, they'll start with the vendor who charges $25 per hour, and if he's not available they'll go to the next vendor who charges $30 per hour, and so forth.

That way they can keep your maintenance and repair bills as low as possible. Ask your property manager how she sources vendors.

Tenant placement fees

Investors shouldn't reject a property management company out-of-hand based on its fee structure alone but should create a side-by-side comparison to help in deciding which property manager to work with. Here's an example.

Exhibit 4.1: Typical Property Management Fee Schedules

Factor	Property Manager X	Property Manager Y	Property Manager Z
Monthly Management Fee	8.0%	9.0%	10.0%
Maintenance	In-house	third-party, no markup	third-party 15% markup
Tenant Placement Fees	80% of first month's rent	50% of first month's rent	None

As you can see, it's not always straightforward to compare one property management company's fees with another's. Some charge lower monthly rates but higher tenant placement fees; others mark up maintenance and others don't.

Other considerations

In-house maintenance gives the property management company an incentive to send work crews out on multiple service calls as a way of generating revenue for the property management company. That doesn't mean they will, but it is an exposure. Others may use a third-party vendor and get a kickback from the vendors they hire.

If the property management company charges tenant placement fees, then they're happy with constant tenant turnover, as they get a lump sum every time a new tenant moves in, plus any revenue from the make-ready (cleaning, painting, repairs) for the new tenant. That's not the incentive you want them to have. The less they depend on tenant placement fees for their income, the better.

Does your property manager own rentals in the same area where you own rentals? In a way, that's good in that it shows they have "skin in the game" by investing in their own market. On the other hand, if you have a vacancy and they have a vacancy at the same time, will they cherry-pick the best tenants for themselves and give you whoever is left over? Of course they will.

The property manager will make money one way or the other, and all pricing models can be abused, so it comes down to whom you can trust. For that, rely on recommendations from other investors in that market, who can be found at local meetup groups or real estate investor associations mentioned earlier. Here's a checklist of the major things to ask your potential property manager:

Exhibit 4.2: Property Manager Checklist

Company	
Years in business	
Number of properties under management	
Software used	
Number of leasing agents	
Fees	
Monthly management fee	
Leasing fee, new tenant	
Leasing fee, renewing tenant	

Markup on repairs	
Other fees	
Late fees kept by owner or property manager?	
Tenant deposit held by owner or property manager?	
Operations	
How often is property inspected?	
In-house handymen? What hourly rate?	
How do you determine fair market rents for an area?	
Markup on third-party maintenance crews?	
24-hour hotline for tenants?	
Is there a single point of contact for the owner?	
Statements available online 24/7?	
Funds deposited to owner's bank by _____ of each month?	
Recommendations on Section 8 tenants	
Recommendations/policies on pets	
Tenant Screening Criteria	
Credit check	
Criminal check	
Income-to-rent ratio	
Contact current and previous landlord?	
Describe eviction process	

In addition to the above, you should get a sense of how well they know their market, for example: What features do tenants look for and value when finding a home to live in? You want a property that will "fly off the shelf" as soon as it's on the market; not one that will take weeks to get rented.

Finally, you should ask for a copy of documents like the Property Management Agreement with Owner and the Lease Agreement with Tenant.

Managing the property manager

As much as it is the property manager's job to manage your property, it's your job to manage the property manager, especially when you first start working together. This is a fine line, because property management is a thankless task: One never-ending stream of problems and complaints about tenants, toilets, and termites. The last thing a veteran property manager wants is a newbie investor who took some weekend seminar and then tries to tell her how to do her job. You have to tread lightly here.

At each step, you should be checking to ensure the property manager is doing what you want done, the way you want it done. Don't assume she is going to do her job well—or at all.

Putting the property on the market

There is nothing more disappointing after a few weeks of vacancy than to go to rental sites online and find out that your property isn't listed, or the number of beds or baths is inaccurate, or that the photos are dark and unclear because they were taken poorly with someone's cell phone.

When your property is listed for rent, immediately check the listings on all the major sites: Rent.com, Realtor.com, Trulia.com, Zillow.com, etc., and ensure that your property is posted and that the text and photos show the property as attractive as possible.

Property managers list dozens of properties, and they'll usually assign the task to a junior member of their team who won't care as much about the listing as you, the owner, will. Many leasing agents will just go through the motions because they've done hundreds of listings. Check the listings on all the sites as soon as your property is marketed and check daily until they're the way you want them. Compare your listing with other properties in the same neighborhood—does your leasing agent make *your* property stand out from the rest?

In conclusion, keep in mind that property management is what will make or break your investment. It's the Achilles heel of investing, especially remote investing. Make sure you get this right.

CHAPTER 5
TENANTS

M ost investors think in terms of neighborhoods and properties first, then look for a tenant almost as an afterthought. I think that's a mistake. The tenant should be at the core of your business model. It's the tenant who will pay off your mortgage for you; it's the tenant who may trash or take good care of your property; it's the tenant who can make your whole business plan break down. So I recommend a tenant-centric approach to investing.

TENANT PROFILE

What is the profile of the tenant you want to rent to and deal with for the next five to ten years? The tenant you define will then dictate the neighborhood and property.

Lifestyle vs. necessity tenants

First, be aware of the difference between "lifestyle tenants" and "tenants-by-necessity."

A lifestyle tenant is one who could buy a home but chooses to rent. She could be a millennial who likes living in a downtown area with shops, restaurants, and bars—all within walking distance of her apartment. She could buy a primary residence in a suburb or residential part of town if she wanted to, but she prefers to live close to amenities offered in the "urban core."

A tenant-by-necessity has lower income and lower credit scores and doesn't have the option of buying a primary residence. This tenant rents because she has no other option. Maybe she's a single mom with three kids, or a recent graduate just starting out.

Lifestyle tenants make better tenants but have a higher risk of leaving. Therefore, it usually doesn't pay to try and squeeze every last dollar of rent from them because these tenants have options. They can easily find another place to rent, or even buy their own homes. So rather than raise the monthly rent $25 after the lease term, it might be more cost-effective to impose a "nuisance increase" of $10 per month. (A "nuisance increase" is one so small that it won't be worth the trouble for the tenant to leave, while at the same time it conditions the tenant to expect an increase each year.)

A tenant-by-necessity may cause more wear-and-tear on the property but tends to move less often due to having fewer options. Due to the additional wear-and-tear, market-rate rent increases might make more sense.

RENT RANGES AND RELATED CONSIDERATIONS

Regardless of which type of tenant you have, you should consult with your property manager and determine what rent range you want to play in, as that will determine the quality of tenant you can attract and therefore what kind of property and neighborhood you should invest in.

For example, in St. Louis there's a distinct cutoff in tenant quality at the $800 mark: Tenants who can afford $800 and above are qualitatively different from tenants who can only afford $600, $650, or $700 per month, and max out at $800 with Section 8.

Lower-rent tenants often live paycheck-to-paycheck, spend more time in the property, and cause more wear-and-tear. They're more likely to have alcohol or substance-abuse problems and may have to be hounded to pay rent (and sometimes are forced by circumstances to pay it in installments throughout the month).

How do I know that $800 is the magic number in that market? I make it a practice to talk to multiple property managers to get the "lay of the land" before ever setting foot in a market. You should too.

So, in our St. Louis example, if I were looking to invest, I would start with the rents: What neighborhoods will command rents of $800 or more? That will determine the type of properties I should be looking for (age, number of bedrooms, baths, etc.) and in what areas. Sure, that eighty-year-old, $45,000 two-bedroom cottage that rents for $600 per month has an attractive rent ratio, but do you really want to be in that business?

The rent ratio may sound high, but the tenant will be unable to pay that rent twelve months in a row. There'll be late payments, no payments, evictions, court appearances, and other headaches. Dealing with these issues is not worth the aggravation in my opinion. Find out from your property management company what the rent cutoff is between tenants who are responsible and accountable vs. those who are less responsible and make excuses for sub-standard performance.

Once you know what that bottom line for higher-quality tenants is for your chosen market—whether it's $800, $900, $1,000—then you know what neighborhoods to focus on (next chapter).

What about Section 8?

Section 8 is a federal program administered by the Department of Housing and Urban Development (HUD) that uses taxpayer dollars to fund some or all of the rent for low-income households. There are approximately five million such households currently in the Section 8 program nationwide.

In some cases, the government will pay the entire rent; in most cases the government will pay a portion and the tenant is responsible for the balance.

The good news about Section 8

The government-subsidized part of the rents is wired electronically to your bank account on the first of each month like clockwork and, so far, has been unaffected by government shutdowns (knock on wood).

It has also been a boon during the Covid-19 pandemic in which many tenants lost their jobs and became unable to pay rent, all while many landlords weren't allowed to evict them! Having that monthly wire transfer from the federal government made surviving the pandemic considerably easier for many investors.

Section 8 rents are often at above-market rates, to compensate landlords for taking in higher-risk tenants. So a given property that may rent for $650 per month might command $700 per month via the Section 8 program.

Dogma Alert!

This is one aspect of the Section 8 program that I resent just on principle. It's disheartening to see a potential tenant get priced out of a home because a Section 8 tenant can bring the owner higher rent. Think of the irony: Taxpayer X, who works for a living, is paying taxes to subsidize a Section 8 tenant, so that the Section 8 tenant can outbid him for the home he wants. That's just wrong in my opinion.

Some property managers have told me that Section 8 tenants stay longer, because the tenants don't want the hassle of dealing with the government in order to move to another home. Section 8 also offers a steady pool of available tenants, even during down times like over the holidays.

The bad news about Section 8

Section 8 often attracts higher-risk tenants, i.e., someone who doesn't have his or her finances or life together. This often results in more wear-and-tear on the property. HUD doesn't pay the security deposit, so the tenant has to. This might actually be a blessing in disguise because it shows that the tenant is at least somewhat financially responsible and capable of saving.

Some tenants have a sense of entitlement and run to the housing authority for every little complaint.

If the Section 8 tenant is moving into your property mid-month, the previous owner may drag his feet with regard to forwarding the pro-rated share of the payments.

War Story

I was once looking to buy a house in a new development in Las Vegas one evening and saw there were police cars down the street; the officers were settling a domestic disturbance. One of the residents I spoke to said that the neighborhood was nice until some Section 8 tenants moved in, and suddenly burglaries and car break-ins started happening. The Section 8 tenants often had domestic squabbles that the police had to be called in for. Needless to say, I decided not to invest in that neighborhood!

Participating in this program is like going into business with the government and is another layer of bureaucracy you have to deal with. To stay in the program, HUD will send inspectors to your property every year to ensure it's compliant with HUD safety and living standards. In most markets, this is at most a minor inconvenience, but has the added benefit of getting a free property inspection each year.

Dogma Alert!

I've had Section 8 tenants in the past and was fortunate not to have major issues with them. But the prospect of working with the government is such that I personally consider renting to Section 8 tenants only as a last resort.

In summary, when deciding whether to accept Section 8 tenants, here are some considerations:

Ask your property manager what her experience has been with Section 8 in their market, and what her recommendation is. If she recommends it, try to ascertain if she's only doing so because it means she doesn't have to work so hard to find a tenant, or if she genuinely thinks it's a good option for you—in which case, have her explain why.

Screen Section 8 tenants just as you would open-market tenants. You don't have to accept everybody. Look for people who are on what I call an "upward trajectory." Maybe the tenant is a single mom with two kids, but she's working and going to night school so she can get a higher-paying job. This is a qualitatively different tenant than a single mom with two kids who is in and out of rehab and has a history of short-term employment. The first applicant on the "upward trajectory" is potentially a good tenant; the second applicant is probably too risky.

On the plus side, in a market like Detroit, which has an economy based on one industry (autos), Section 8 tenants might be a way to mitigate your risk of owning property in a market that can get hit harder during an economic downturn. Recession or no recession, the government pays the rent, or at least most of it.

Is the area where you're considering investing a Section 8 neighborhood? If there are a lot of other Section 8 tenants in the area, your Section 8 tenants could fit quite well. But if not—e.g., if it's a white picket-fence suburban area—then Section 8 tenants could potentially stick out and cause resentment among the neighbors.

Animals

Pets are your tenants too. Should you allow them in your property?

Two-thirds of US households have either a dog or a cat, so having a no-pet policy will significantly reduce your pool of available tenants. I've also heard anecdotally that people with pets don't move as often because it's harder for them to find another house that accepts pets. The longer the tenant stays, the better for you. On the other hand, pets can cause damage.

Here are some guidelines:

No dangerous breeds. Most property managers will recommend not allowing dangerous breeds like pit bulls or Dobermans. Laws vary from one market to another, so check with your property manager to see what she recommends, and how it's addressed in the rental agreement.

Extra rent: If you do allow pets, you should charge a non-refundable pet fee ($200-$500) to cover the expected cleanup after the tenant leaves; consider also adding $25 or more to the monthly rent. Again, consult with your property manager.

Cats can leave smells behind that are difficult to remove. In one of my Phoenix houses, disinfecting the garage floor didn't work, nor did using an enzyme cleanser. Eventually I had to have the surface covered with a shellac-based sealer called Zinsser to cover the smell. Getting cat smells out of carpeting can also be difficult, and costly.

Check with your property manager to see what effect pets may have on your ability to rent. If you're in a slow market or time of year, you may want to allow pets. But if not allowing pets only means it'll take longer to find a tenant, then it might be worth the wait. Check with your property manager and decide from there.

Dogma Alert!

If it's a new-construction home, I prefer not to allow pets of any kind. The property is in pristine condition and the downsides of allowing pets are significant. If it's a renovated home, I'll allow dogs as long as they're not dangerous breeds, but not cats. That's just my preference and is by no means universal among investors.

Extra for Experts: A Word about Lease-to-Own Contracts

With regard to tenants, one thing you'll hear about is Lease-to-Own Contracts. Here's how they work: You rent your property to a tenant, but the tenant has the option of buying the property from you at an agreed-upon price after a certain number of years, usually within five. In exchange for that option, the tenant pays a premium, such as an extra $100 per month that goes into an escrow account for the down payment. If the tenant chooses to exercise that option, he or she buys the property from you at the agreed-upon price.

This is typically done by having two separate documents, one for the rental contract and another for the sales contract.

The lease-option can be appealing to you, the investor, for a few reasons:

- The tenant is more likely to take care of the property since she hopes to own it someday.

- You receive an extra $100 per month and get to keep it if the tenant doesn't exercise the purchase option.

- In reality, fewer than 10% of tenants who sign lease-to-buy contracts actually do buy.

The downside is that it's harder to evict such tenants if they fail to pay the rent. Even if you have two separate documents for rental and for purchase, it's quite possible a judge will rule that the tenant has an equity ownership claim due to the option money she's paid, thereby requiring a foreclosure rather than a simple eviction. This can turn a one-month eviction process into a six-month foreclosure process, depending on what state the property is in.

In summary:

- Consult with your property manager

- Identify the type(s) of tenants you're targeting

- That will determine the neighborhoods and properties you should be looking for

CHAPTER 6
NEIGHBORHOOD

Any discussion of neighborhoods has to begin with standard definitions used in the industry. While there are no strict definitions, neighborhoods are classified as "A," "B," "C," or "D" in real estate investing.

Definitions

An "A" neighborhood is the best neighborhood, where doctors, lawyers, and engineers live; they have good schools, low crime, and are almost all owner-occupied. These neighborhoods tend to be more expensive and therefore don't cash flow very well. Investors generally don't invest in them unless they think the areas are going to appreciate significantly; such investing for future appreciation is speculative and therefore riskier.

A "B" neighborhood is where working class people live: nurses, schoolteachers, police, fire fighters. They tend to have decent schools, low levels of crime, and while they are predominantly owner-occupied, some houses on the street will have renters.

A "C" neighborhood is one with lower quality schools, more crime, and typically populated more by renters than homeowners. The homes tend to cash flow very well on paper because the prices are low relative to rents, so investors can potentially get good cash flow. But "C" neighborhoods also attract lower quality tenants and have higher maintenance expenses because those tenants don't take as good care of the property. You're also somewhat at the mercy of your next-door neighbor. You may take care of your property and maintain it well, but your next-door neighbor might be a slumlord, where junk cars and trash pile up in the yard. That affects what quality of tenant you can attract and what kind of rents you can command.

Often, these "cash flow" houses are in reality "trash flow" houses, because of higher property management fees (10%), higher repair and maintenance expenses, and missed rents. Such houses can still work for you if they're in the city where you live and you can manage them yourself—i.e., collect the rents and make repairs yourself, etc. Otherwise, these "C" properties and the tenants who rent them are too high-maintenance to fit the passive income model.

A "D" neighborhood is basically a war zone. This is where you have graffiti, boarded-up houses, barbed wire, drug dealers on street corners, and drive-by shooters. Typically, investors do not invest in "D" neighborhoods.

A real-estate insiders' joke is that for you to visit your property in a "D" neighborhood you'll need to bring a gun, whereas to visit your property in a "C" neighborhood you'll only need to bring a knife. Humor aside, investors should avoid "D" neighborhoods unless they are highly experienced and have a strategy for making properties like those work.

Another way to think of the classifications is that "A" stands for appreciation, "C" stands for cash flow, and "B" stands for a little of both. For most investors, the "B" neighborhood is the sweet spot. "A" neighborhoods don't cash flow and "C" neighborhoods cash flow on paper, but as we've seen, in real life tend to create more headaches for the owners.

In a sweet-spot "B" neighborhood, most occupants are owners who have pride of ownership, take care of their homes, mow their lawns, keep them clean and in good repair; if you own one of two rentals on the street, the value of your property is protected.

War Story

Since there are no firm definitions for where a "B" neighborhood ends and a "C" neighborhood begins, many sellers will claim their property is a "B" property in a "B" neighborhood when in fact it's a "C." Buyer beware.

I'm going to put a stake in the ground and create my own industry definitions. To me the critical criteria is: What percent of the occupants in an area are renters versus homeowners? The higher the percentage of homeowners, the better. Why? Homeowners have pride of ownership and take care of their property. As a group, tenants don't take care of a property as well.

So I define a "B" neighborhood as one with a preponderance of owners over renters. At a minimum, I prefer a two-to-one ratio of homeowners to renters (and preferably more, say 70% owners and 30% tenants). I define a "C" neighborhood as one with more tenants than owners.

Due to zoning, most cities have "high-density housing" areas, with a mix of apartments, fourplexes, and rental homes. These neighborhoods are—or are likely to become—"C" neighborhoods.

The distinction between "B" and "C" is significant for reasons mentioned previously, and summarized here as your property value, tenant quality, and exit strategy:

Your Property Value

A well-maintained neighborhood with manicured lawns will preserve your property value. Homeowners have pride of ownership and want to take care of their homes. That means your house will be surrounded by other nice houses. Tenants, however, generally don't take care of a home the way a homeowner would. If you're in a tenant neighborhood, your property may not appreciate, or might even drop in value.

Tenant Quality

A "C" neighborhood will attract "C" tenants, not just yours but those of your neighbors. I've had very good tenants who wanted to terminate the lease because the neighbor behind them was always drunk and noisy. It's discouraging to take the time to maintain your property, attract good tenants, and then be at the mercy of your next-door neighbor, who's a slumlord.

Your "C" tenants are more likely to be living paycheck-to-paycheck, and most likely to have difficulty paying rent when times are bad, or there's disruption like with the Coronavirus. They may be able to pay the rent, but often not twelve consecutive months.

Exit Strategy

If you're in an owner neighborhood, you have three exit strategies: Sell to your tenant if she wants to buy, sell to another investor, or sell to an owner-occupant on MLS. Typically, you can get a higher price from the owner-occupant because for them it's an emotional decision, whereas for an investor, it's just about the numbers. By contrast, if you're in a tenant neighborhood you have only one exit strategy: Sell to another investor. And a fellow investor is looking at it solely in terms of dollars and cents and will drive a harder bargain.

You can find this information through online resources such as City-Data.com or Niche.com. You go to the site and key in the city name (or better yet, the zip code of the property you're considering buying).

In the example below, I went to Niche.com and typed in the zip code 35810, which is in Huntsville, Alabama.

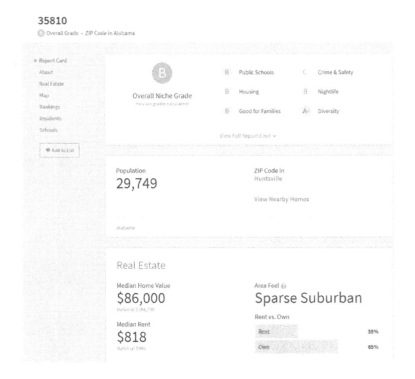

Niche.com rates this as a "B" neighborhood ("Overall Niche Grade") and provides stats about the area.

As you can see, one of the statistics on that zip code is the percentage of renters versus owners, and there are twice as many owners as there are renters, which is what I like to see. I personally wouldn't buy in an area with the percentage of renters more than 35%, but many other investors do.

Tip

Whenever I buy a property, I take a screenshot of the Niche. com page for that zip code and save it in my property folder. Years later, I can check Niche.com again and see if the neighborhood has turned: Is the area deteriorating, getting better, or about the same? There's no way I'm going to remember all the stats years later, so saving this page gives me a snapshot of the neighborhood at the time I purchased the property. You might want to do this as well, as a best practice.

Things to Evaluate from Your Desktop

It bears repeating: If you fly out every time you're considering a prospective market, you'll waste time and money on travel expenses to places that don't work out. It's far better to do most of your research on your computer and eliminate 90% of the markets you're considering, and then visit in-person only the "short list" of the most promising markets.

Recommended resources

> City-Data.com
> Niche.com
> Neighborhood360.com
> GoodSchools.org
> NeighborhoodScout.com
> CrimeReports.com

Schools

Of course, a good school district is more desirable than a bad one. The better schools will attract higher quality tenants and homes in those districts generally rent faster. Also, once a family moves into such a home, they tend not to move as often once their kids are enrolled in the school district. A win all around, right?

Not necessarily. You shouldn't expect to find cash flow property in the highest-rated school districts. The highest-rated school districts will generally be in "A" neighborhoods that are too expensive to cash flow. A school rating of six or seven on a ten-point scale is more realistic for a cash flow property.

And there are exceptions! Some high-end neighborhoods in the country have sub-standard schools, because many residents send their kids to private school and the public schools are under-funded. I heard of one school in Texas that had lousy ratings, yet some parents still wanted their kids to go there. Why? Because the school has a good athletic program and students often get scholarships to a college or university. Go figure.

So start with areas that cash flow, and then seek out the best schools you can find within those areas.

Rent level

You can ask your property manager or investors at the local REIA if there's a rent level you don't want to go below. As mentioned in the chapter on Tenants, in St. Louis, one property manager I spoke with said he only buys in neighborhoods that can command rents of $800 per month or higher; lower than $800 will get you a lower-quality tenant who's living paycheck-to-paycheck and whose payments may be sporadic.

In other cities, the cutoff could be higher or lower. Ask your property manager what rent levels you should be considering *before* you go shopping for properties.

Household income (HHI) by zip code

We already discussed the advantages of investing in a predominately owner-occupied neighborhood: Owners take care of their properties and therefore the neighborhoods look better and preserve their market value.

To expand on that concept, you should also look at the ratio of household income (HHI) vs. housing prices, as it provides a clue as to whether an area has appreciation potential. A general rule is that a home buyer can qualify for a loan that's three times the HHI. So, a household with income of $50,000 per year could afford a home as high as $150,000. So, if you can find an area where the average household income is $50,000 and the average home price is only $100,000, that area has potential to appreciate because the people there have incomes that can support rising prices. Note that this is just one data point, and not a guarantee that such appreciation will in fact happen!

Education level

Related to household income is education level. What percent of residents in a given neighborhood have college degrees, advanced degrees, or high school diplomas? The higher the education level, the better. You can find educational level by zip code at Niche.com.

Freeways

How close are the properties you're considering to major freeways? That will enable you to recruit tenants from a larger area, as tenants can jump on the freeways and commute farther to work. Also, companies looking to expand in an area often locate their factories, offices, etc., close to freeways, so that could improve your chances of additional local job growth.

Proximity to services

If the property you're considering is close to churches and schools, that's a plus. Churches and schools get more police "drive-bys" and generally have less crime. Being close to services such as grocery stores, strip malls, and childcare are all a plus. Being within walking distance of public transportation routes is especially important in lower-income neighborhoods ("C") or in climates with lots of cold weather and snow. Being able to walk to the bus stop or train station greatly simplifies the lives of your tenants and you'll be able to fill vacancies more quickly.

You can determine proximity to services by looking at the neighborhood's "Walk Score," available on www.Redfin. com, one of the major real estate sites. You simply go to the site, type in the zip code of the property you're considering, and it'll give you scores for walkability, public transit, and bike-friendliness. As an example, here's a score for a zip code where I used to go to school:

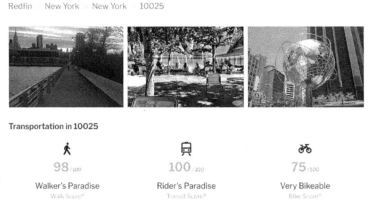

As you can see, that neighborhood gets perfect or near-perfect scores for walkability and public transportation, and very high scores for being "bikeable."

Downside risk

Talk to your property manager about what happens in the metro during tough times. How did this area fare in previous crashes, like in 2008? How will it fare in the next crash? Real estate is a long-term investment and it's likely you'll experience a recession during the time you own it.

THINGS TO EVALUATE IN-PERSON

Crime

You can evaluate crime statistics from some of the afore-mentioned data sources and eliminate right off the bat any neighborhoods with high crime rates. Especially important is to focus on violent crime vs. property crime. Property crimes like burglary or car break-ins are bad enough, but violent crime like muggings and home invasions will drive tenants away.

Even for neighborhoods that websites say are safe, you should double-check when you visit in-person. When I visit a market, for instance, I take a rental car and drive through the neighborhoods I'm considering on weekend nights. Most neighborhoods look fine during the day when the real estate agent is driving you around. But if anything bad is going to happen, it's more likely to be on a Friday or Saturday night. That's typically when domestic disturbances happen, and in the worst neighborhoods, when drug dealing and prostitution activities are evident. After the real estate agent is done with her dog-and-pony show, I'll get in my rental car and drive through those same neighborhoods at night to confirm that what I'm being told is accurate.

Note: This is true for "C" neighborhoods and I would also check on "B" neighborhoods to make sure. "A" neighborhoods don't need this step.

Curb appeal

While visiting a neighborhood, also keep an eye out for the quality of the cars in the driveways and streets. Are there a lot of clunkers and old vehicles? Or are they mostly well-maintained, late-model cars? Are the lawns well-manicured? Do the neighbors have junk, bicycles, or basketball hoops in front of their houses? Are there boarded-up houses, or houses in need of repair? What quality of tenant can you expect to attract in the neighborhood you're considering? What you want to see is pride of ownership, where the neighborhood takes care of itself.

Sub-markets

In some cities like Kansas City, MO, neighborhoods can vary drastically from block to block. You could be in a decent neighborhood, but two blocks in one direction is a ghetto and two blocks in the opposite direction contains high-end homes. Modern communities are planned, but in older cities on the East Coast and in the Midwest, there is less master planning and neighborhoods tend to have "evolved" in certain ways.

Along the East Coast in particular, there are identifiable changes in neighborhoods: The Italian neighborhoods, the Irish neighborhoods, the Black neighborhoods, Chinatown, and others. This is because when the waves of immigrants came to the East Coast cities in the 1800s, they wanted to be with each other. For example, the Italians all spoke Italian and wanted to be with other Italian immigrants with whom they shared common language, churches, customs, and food. The same was true for other ethnic groups as well. The character of those neighborhoods are much the same today.

Personally, when growing up in Philadelphia, I had an unconscious awareness of where my neighborhood ended and the other guy's neighborhood began. There were no signs or other markers—everyone just *knew*. As an outsider visiting these areas looking for investment property, you should develop that awareness too.

Gentrification

One thing you'll come across are areas that are "gentrifying" e.g., a "C" neighborhood that's turning into a "B" or "A" neighborhood. Often, these are urban core locations where a formerly rundown area starts becoming trendy with millennials, new cafes, restaurants, pubs, etc. If you come across such an area, you have the possibility of buying a low-priced property and have it appreciate as rental demand grows. This appreciation can take ten or more years, but it does happen.

The problem is that almost everyone who's trying to sell you a "C" property will tell you that this area is "gentrifying" and therefore you should buy it—and even pay a premium for it! Take these claims with a grain of salt, because not all "C" or "B" neighborhoods can be gentrifying!

What are the factors that can help you identify areas most likely to gentrify?

- Job growth, such as new employers (especially technology, health care, and financial services) opening in an area, attracting higher-income employees and residents

- Walkability, i.e., featuring services or amenities within walking distance

- Easy access to public transportation

- New cafes and pubs appearing

- Ask real estate agents if they're starting to see multiple offers on properties, properties selling above asking price, or days-on-market declining. Those are signs of a market that's heating up.

- Go to the City Planning Commission website and see if permits have been issued for commercial projects, such as conversions of old warehouses into lofts, or conversions of apartment buildings into condominiums.

- See if you can identify areas with a large price disparity between an up-and-coming neighborhood and those surrounding it.

An example of the latter is the San Francisco Bay Area in the last few years, where home prices had risen to astronomical levels. For example, a three-bedroom, two-bath, 1,400 square foot row home could cost $1.5 million dollars. But right across the bay—just a short train ride away—the same house in Oakland was going for $500,000.

Nature abhors a vacuum. When there's such a price disparity, people will buy where it's cheaper and commute into the city for work, and that's what happened. In Oakland, homes within walking distance of a Bay Area Rapid Transit (BART) station doubled in value within five years.

If you're going to bank on gentrification, understand that this increases your risk. Make sure the property you buy is cash-flow positive and is a sound investment even if the gentrification doesn't happen: Ten years is a long time to hold a non-performing asset! Any upside due to gentrification is a riskier bet and should be looked at as "icing on the cake."

In the end this is a judgment call, so collect as many data points as possible before you decide.

In summary:

- Consult with your property manager

- Research neighborhoods online to eliminate ones you're not interested in

- Tour the area, either in-person or virtually

CHAPTER 7
PRO FORMAS

Turnkey providers and other sellers will provide you with financial statements called pro formas, which are projections of how the property will perform financially after you purchase it. As with all projections, you should take these with a grain of salt because it's in their interest to make the property look as financially appealing as possible.

If you're buying the property off the MLS, then you'll have to generate these estimates on your own. The exhibit below shows the typical pro forma provided by a turnkey provider. We will now go through the numbers line-by-line so you'll be able to do your due diligence and make adjustments when the projections are not accurate or realistic. In this case, your turnkey provider or local real estate agent gives you the following projections, which make the property look like a tempting investment: 22.5% cash-on-cash returns!

Exhibit 7.1: Pro Forma Financial Statement

123 Main St. Memphis TN	Pro Forma
Selling Price	100,000
Down Payment	20,000
Closing Costs @2.5%	2,500
All-in Acquisition Cost	**22,500**
Rent	1,050
Mortgage Payment @5.0%	(434)
Property Taxes	(60)
Insurance	(50)
Property Management @8.0%	(84)
	-
	-
Total Expenses	**(628)**
Monthly Cash Flow	422
Annual Cash Flow	5,064
Cash-on-Cash Return	**22.5%**
(Annual Cash Flow/Acq Cost)	

Obviously the seller wants to make the investment look as good as possible in order to make the sale. How can you tell if these projections are believable? Go line-by-line and do a reality check on the assumptions, correcting anything you think is overly optimistic, and then come up with your own pro forma. Happily, this is a pretty straightforward process, which we'll go into now.

Selling price

When you get a property appraisal later in this process, you'll have confirmation that the selling price is fair, but you should do a sanity check at the outset so you don't spend too much time on a deal that's overpriced.

This is easily done by checking property sites online, such as Realtor.com, Trulia.com, Zillow.com, Redfin.com, and others. Type in the zip code of the property and then use the site's filters to find properties with the same number of bedrooms and baths, square footage, and other traits.

You'll find a range of $90,000-$110,000 in our example, which lets you know up front that the quote price is in the ballpark. If the sale price is at the high end of the range, make it your business to understand why. Maybe it has just been renovated with stainless appliances and granite counters.

Down payment

Assuming the selling price is reasonable, the down payment is usually 20% of that price. You can leave that in the pro forma, or you could ask your lender for a quote for what your interest rate would be if you put 25% down. You may choose to put a little more down payment in order to lock in lower rates. See Chapter 9: Financing for more details.

Closing costs

Many closing costs are fixed, i.e. the same whether it's a $100,000 house or a $500,000 house. That means that for lower-priced homes, the closing costs may be higher as a percentage of the purchase price. In our example, $2,500 seems low for a financed closing. Get an estimate of closing costs from your lender and use that in your calculations.

Rent

The seller has an interest in making the rent projections as optimistic as possible and often overstates the rent. To do a reality check on the rent projections, go through the same process you used to confirm the purchase price: Go to the aforementioned websites, type in the zip code, square footage, number of bedrooms and baths, and see what similar properties actually rent for in that market.

These sites can give you a range, but the figures are not gospel. What you're looking for here is, "Is the projected rent realistic?" You'll typically find that there's a range for properties similar to yours; for example, rents could be anywhere from $800 to $1,000 a month. If the rent your provider is projecting is at the high end of the range, ask yourself: "Why would a tenant pay above average rent for that property?" Has it been rehabbed to a very high standard, with granite countertops and luxury vinyl tile flooring? Is it in a better location? If so, then the rent projections may be realistic.

Dogma Alert!

Be careful about trying to squeeze every last dollar of rent from tenants. The best tenants—those with good work histories, stable jobs, and references—have many options. By trying to get top dollar, those best tenants may rent elsewhere, and you'll attract the next lower tier of tenants. It's better to leave $25-50 on the table and get the property rented quickly, in my opinion.

Another thing to check for is how many other rentals are on the market in that same zip code. If there are fifty other properties for rent in the same zip code, you're going to have a lot of competition for tenants. When there are too many vacant properties and not enough tenants, your property will either remain vacant for a longer time or you'll have to slash the rent.

Finally, consider the time of year the property is going on the rental market. Typically, it's harder to find tenants over the holidays (Thanksgiving, Christmas, New Year's), so to attract a tenant during that time of year, you may have to lower the rents.

Tenant applications usually pick up noticeably in February:

- The holidays are over.

- Many tenants get their tax refunds from the IRS and use it for rent and security deposits.

- In some markets (Dallas, Pittsburgh), wives can't get their husbands to look at houses on the weekends as long as football season is on. After the Super Bowl (usually the first Sunday in February), rental activity picks up.

So if your property is on the market over the holidays, you may need to lower the rent projections in your pro forma or make an allowance for a month or two of vacancy.

Dogma Alert!

If you have someone applying to rent your property in the dead of winter with four feet of snow on the ground, you might even get suspicious. Maybe they have a good explanation for why they're in the market during blizzard-like conditions, but it's also possible they have some issues (e.g., recent eviction) that compels them to be looking for housing at that time of year. Check references carefully.

Another way to do a sanity check on the projected rents is to make an onsite visit to the market. Pretend you're looking to rent a property and check out the competition by finding other properties similar to yours that are for rent and see what you're competing against. Is your property better or worse than the one you're thinking of buying? If your property has been rehabbed to a really high standard vs. the competition, the higher rent projection may be justified.

In summary, the property provider's projections are based on averages, and while they may be accurate in general, you may want to adjust the projected rent down (and length of vacancy) to account for the time of year. Conversely, a property going on the market in spring or, even better, in the summer when the kids aren't in school will likely rent faster and your rent may actually be higher than what's projected.

So, going to these websites is good for getting a reality check and for understanding what's on the market and whether the rent projections you've been getting are realistic. Based on what you're seeing through your online research, you should make your own adjustments to the projected rents. If you think the projected rent of $1,000 per month is too optimistic, reduce it to $900 or $950 and see if the investment still makes sense for you.

Vacancy

Some turnkey providers don't even include an estimate for vacancy—and that's unrealistic. Sooner or later your property will be vacant, and you have to account for that in your financial projections. A good rule of thumb is to use 5% as a vacancy reserve. This implies that your property will be vacant one month out of every year and a half. Check with your property management company on what a realistic expectation is for the average number of months that tenants stay. In many markets, tenants stay for two and a half years on average so you can count on one month of vacancy for every thirty months.

If your property is in a "C" neighborhood or is a multifamily like a duplex, triplex, or fourplex, you might want to increase the vacancy estimate to 7.5%. That's because these types of properties typically have higher turnover, and you can assume the tenants will leave after one year. If it takes a month to do the make-ready (clean the carpets, freshen the paint, repair any damage) and find a new tenant, that means you'll have one month of vacancy every thirteen months. One divided by thirteen comes out to 7.69%, which is ridiculously precise for what is essentially a "finger-in-the-air" estimate, so I recommend using a 7.5% vacancy rate for "C" neighborhoods or multifamily properties.

Note: Section 8 tenants tend to stay longer because it's such a hassle dealing with the government to get vouchers moved from one property to another. You can check with the property manager in your market to find out how long such tenants stay, on average.

Another "gotcha" is tenant placement fees. When there's a vacancy, some property managers will charge one month's rent to advertise, screen, and place a new tenant. That's another month of lost rent! So if on average a tenant stays for two years and leaves, you'll lose one month's rent for doing the make-ready (new paint, carpets, cleaning) and another month for the tenant placement fee. So in a twenty-six-month period, you'll have twenty-four months of rents and two months of no rent. That equates to 7.69% economic vacancy (= 2/26).

Principal, interest

Ask your lender for financing options if you put 25% down instead of 20%. Most turnkey providers base their projections on a 20% down payment, but the more you put down, the lower your rate will be. The lower rates usually plateau at 25% down, so whether you put 25% down or 50% down, it doesn't matter: After 25%, the rate will often be the same.

So, is it better to put more principal down and get the lower rate or to conserve your capital and take a higher rate? That depends in part on how long you intend to hold the property. As a rule of thumb, the longer you hold the property the more advantageous it will be to have a lower interest rate, so if you're going to hold it for a long time it may be worth putting 25% down instead of 20% down and adjust the financial projections accordingly.

Dogma Alert!

In my experience, most investors hold property longer than they anticipate. Real estate is not a liquid asset, and you may buy a property thinking you're going to sell in five years but who knows what market conditions will be five years from now? You may very well wind up owning the property a lot longer than you think, so you may want to err on the side of going for the lower interest rate.

Property taxes

The next item on the pro forma is property taxes.

When you see the property tax estimate on the pro forma, you can check it by going to the county tax assessor's website, typing in the address and/or parcel number, and seeing what property taxes were paid in previous years. Most times the pro forma will be accurate, but sometimes someone can make a typo and provide misleading information. It's your job to "trust, but verify."

A second check is to make sure what the projected property taxes would be based on the new sales price, i.e. the price that you're paying for the property and not for the original acquisition price at the time the seller bought it.

So for example, if the seller bought it for $100,000, put $30,000 worth of work into it, and then sells it to you for $150,000, the property taxes shown may very well be based on the $100,000 price the seller originally paid, not the $150,000 price that you're paying. You can go to the county tax assessor's website to find out how they calculate property taxes and make an adjustment to be sure you have a realistic property tax assumption in your pro forma.

Finally, while there, you should investigate how the county assesses taxes and how often they change. Is the tax assessment done annually or every couple of years? This will give you a good idea of what your tax liability will be for the foreseeable future.

Insurance

Often, turnkey providers will give a lowball estimate to insure the house based on the minimal coverage necessary as required by the lender. This may or may not be the level of coverage that you want for your property. You should call the local insurance company and get a quote for what kind of coverage they recommend, and how much that coverage would cost you, and then compare that to what's on the pro forma.

One thing to pay special attention to is flood insurance. A lot of homeowners in Houston had lots of flood damage even though their property was not in a designated flood zone. Many flood zone maps were made decades ago and may not be applicable today.

A good resource is the First Street Foundation, a non-profit with a team of 70+ PhDs who build models to predict flooding. As explained on their home page https://FirstStreet.org: "Flood Factor is a free, online tool that makes it easy to learn if a property has flooded from major events in the past, is currently at risk, and how that risk changes over time. Flood Factor simplifies flooding so anyone can find their risk, understand the science, and make informed decisions to prepare for the future."

Just visit https://floodfactor.com/ and type in the address of the property you're considering and see how much flood risk their model predicts. Realtor.com uses their data to inform buyers of flood risk, which is good enough for me. If the property you're considering has high flood risk, you may want to pass on it. If it has low flood risk, you may choose to buy it but want to get additional flood insurance. In that case, you'd adjust the "Insurance Expense" line on the property pro forma.

Aside from flood insurance, another consideration is an umbrella insurance policy to cover you in the event of lawsuits or other liabilities. Some investors use entities like LLCs for asset protection, but another option is to get an umbrella insurance policy: A $1 million insurance policy costs about $200 a year, and if you ever need to use it, you'll find that it's money well-spent, considering lawyers' fees are often $400 per hour.

Caveat: Insurance companies make their money by selling you insurance, so they'll say you need all kinds of insurance and give you a high estimate. A way to get a realistic level of insurance coverage is to ask the insurance company what the most common claims in that market are. How often do they get claims for hurricanes, hailstorms, or floods? Those are the kinds of things you need to insure yourself against. If they don't get such claims often, they may be recommending more coverage than you really need.

The other resource is other investors. You can ask them what coverage they recommend or ask your insurance company to give you referrals of other investors in that market whom you can talk to.

The bottom line on insurance is that you should take the insurance estimate the turnkey provider puts on the pro forma and adjust it for the level of insurance coverage that YOU want.

Property management expense

Unless the properties you're investing in are in the same town where you live and you plan on managing them yourself, you'll need to hire a property management company. The going rate for property management is 8% to 10% of collected rents each month. In other words, if the rent is $1,000 a month, you'll pay $80 to $100 a month for the property management. If the property you're buying is a new-construction home in a new development, property management might be as low as 6% because such homes are under builder warranty and require less maintenance.

A good property management estimate would be 8% of collected rents if you're in an "A" or a "B" neighborhood, or 10% of collected rents if you're in a "C" neighborhood or own multi-units like duplexes and fourplexes. The reasons for the higher rates include:

- "C" neighborhoods and multifamilies have higher turnover and usually more wear-and-tear on the property and are therefore harder to manage.

- "C" tenants are lower-quality, and the property manager may wind up visiting the property several times during the month to collect rents in installments.

- "C" properties have lower rents. If the rent is $600 per month, you're not going to get quality property management for $48/month (8% of $600).

Maintenance and CapEx

What's the difference between maintenance and CapEx?

Maintenance is for small day-to-day items that are expensed each year, like changing the batteries in the smoke detector or fixing a toilet or putting in a new garbage disposal. Capital expenditures—CapEx for short—are for bigger-ticket items whose expenses are amortized over a number of years, such as a new roof.

A good estimate for maintenance is 5% of collected rents or $50 a month for a property renting for $1,000 a month. This $50 is not taken out of your cash flow, but it's good to set it aside for a rainy day because sooner or later you will have some maintenance expenses.

CapEx is trickier to estimate. If you bought the property right, the five major systems (foundation, roof, HVAC, electrical, and plumbing) should be good for five to ten years. If you didn't do your due diligence, then you may have a major expense looming. Another consideration is age: If you bought a new-construction home, your CapEx should be zero the first year because the property is still under the builder's warranty. After year one, CapEx should still be negligible compared to that of a 100-year-old home in Pittsburgh.

To estimate CapEx, you have to do a "bottom-up" analysis, in which you take the cost of a roof (say $5,000) and then divide it by twenty-five years to come up with an annual reserve for a new roof. This approach can be tedious considering it would have to be done for all of the major systems, plus major appliances and unforeseen events like hailstorms or tree removal. Here's an example below.

Exhibit 7.2: Sample CapEx Calculation

Capital Expense ("CapEx")	Replacement Cost	Lifetime (years)	Cost-per-Year	Cost-per-Month
Carpet	$2,000	5	$400	$33.33
Paint	$2,500	5	$500	$41.67
Appliances	$2,000	10	$200	$16.67
Water Heater	$600	10	$60	$5.00
Garage Door	$1,000	10	$100	$8.33
HVAC	$4,000	15	$267	$22.22
Roof	$6,000	25	$240	$20.00
TOTAL	**$18,100**		**$1,767**	**$147.22**

So in this example, you would want to add $147.22—let's call it $150—per month to your pro forma to get a more realistic view of how this property will perform.

Another way to estimate CapEx is to use a "top-down" approach: A rule of thumb some investors use is to assume 1% of the property value per year for CapEx. So a property valued at $175,000 would have a CapEx of $1,750 per year to maintain, or $145.83 per month.

The top-down is a rough estimate only: Replacing a roof might cost $6,000, and it doesn't matter if the roof is on a $100,000 home or a $200,000 home—the cost of replacing the roof is the same (assuming the two houses are the same size). This top-down approach is good enough for newer homes— say ten years or newer—but for older homes, the bottom-up analysis would provide a much more accurate estimate.

The bottom line is that many properties don't cash flow as well as projected because items like CapEx are omitted because they're too difficult to estimate across-the-board. One way or another, you should make an allowance for CapEx in your calculations.

For older homes—like 80- or 100-year-old homes in the Midwest—you might find that the rent covers the expenses, CapEx and principal paydown, and the bulk of your returns will come when you own the property free-and-clear, after paying off the loans.

Cash flow

Your monthly cash flow is the net rents (rents after an allowance for vacancy) minus all your expenses: principal, interest, taxes, insurance, property management, maintenance, and CapEx. Your annual cash flow is simply the monthly cash flow multiplied by twelve.

Cash-on-cash return (CCR)

Your cash-on-cash return is your annual cash flow divided by the amount you invested in the property, which is your down payment plus your closing costs.

Exhibit 7.3 shows the original pro forma, the adjustments made by the savvy investor (you) as part of her due diligence process, and a revised pro forma that reflects the changes.

Exhibit 7.3: Pro Forma Financial Statement (revised)

123 Main St. Memphis TN	Original Pro Forma	Investor's Adjustments	Revised Pro Forma
Selling Price	100,000	0	100,000
Down Payment	20,000	5,000	25,000
Closing Costs @2.5%	2,500	0	2,500
All-in Acquisition Cost	22,500	5,000	27,500
Rent	1,050	-50	1,000
Vacancy Reserve @ 5.0%	-	-50	(50)
Mortgage Payment @4.0%	(434)	77	(357)
Property Taxes	(60)	-20	(80)
Insurance	(50)	-10	(60)
Property Management @8.0%	(84)	4	(80)
Maintenance @5.0%	-	-50	(50)
CapEx@ 5.0%	-	-50	(50)
Total Expenses	(628)	-99	(727)
Monthly Cash Flow	422		273
Annual Cash Flow	5,064		3,276
Cash-on-Cash Return	22.5%		11.9%
(Annual Cash Flow/Acq Cost)			

Notes on the Adjustments

Down Payment — Decided to put an additional 5% down to get a lower interest rate

Rent — After reviewing comparable rents online, took rent down to be conservative

Vacancy — Original pro forma had no allowance for vacancy

Mortgage Payment — Loan amount is lower due to putting 25% down, causing the interest rate to be 4.0% instead of 5.0%

Property Taxes — Taxes were based on the property value before rehab and will be higher now

Insurance — Conversation with insurance agent resulted in getting a little more coverage

Property Management — Adjusted the amount due to slightly lower rent assumption

Maintenance — Original pro forma had no allowance for maintenance

CapEx — Original pro forma had no allowance for CapEx. In this example, the house received a complete ("gut") rehab so CapEx is estimated at $50 per month.

Note that after our adjustments, the cash-on-cash return on the investment is almost halved, from 22.5% to 11.9%. Does that mean you shouldn't buy the property? Not at all. Double-digit returns are good. But at least now you're going into the investment with your eyes open and know what to expect. Any surprises will likely be to the upside.

Leasing fees were not included in the adjustments since they depend on your property manager's fee schedule and your average tenant stay. For example, if the leasing fee is a month's rent and your average tenant stays one year, that could add $81.25 ($1,000 rent/12 months) to your monthly pro forma. On the other hand, if your property manager charges a 50% leasing fee, or if your tenant stay is longer, your adjustment will be lower.

The same is true for CapEx. If you have a new-construction home still under builder warranty, your CapEx reserve might be close to zero. If you own a 100-year-old rehabbed home in Buffalo, NY, then your CapEx reserve should be higher.

As the investor, you must make some judgments; the thought process above is the best way to approach it.

CHAPTER 8
PROPERTY

As we have stated previously, before shopping for proper-ties, get a reality check from your property manager to help you decide what kind of property you should be getting. You'd be surprised how many investors buy the property first and then consult the property manager afterwards, almost as an afterthought.

Following are vital property attributes to include in your exploration.

THE "NEIGHBORHOOD NORMAL"

There are many older homes in Ohio that have only one bathroom. California investors always have trouble with that: Why would anyone rent a three- or four-bedroom house with only one bathroom? But many of those cities were built in the 1950s and that's what was built; it's normal for locals. People in Cleveland or Detroit might ask Californians, "Why do you need two (or three) bathrooms?"

When shopping for an investment property, adjust your expectations so that they're in line with the "neighborhood normal" for your market.

Middle-of-the-Road Property

In some micro-markets, there's a wide range of properties available. In certain neighborhoods in Kansas City, for example, you could rent small two-bedroom, one-bath cottages for $650 per month, and then a few blocks down the street have a six-bedroom, 4,000 square feet mansion for $3,500 per month.

Your best bet in a market is to avoid the outliers. As an investment, that mansion might look good, but when there's a recession or the market is slow, it'll be much harder to rent and eventually harder to sell. Buy middle-of-the-road properties that have mass appeal to a large rental and buyer pool.

Basements and Garages

One of the reasons many tenants prefer to rent a house instead of an apartment is that houses can offer basements and garages.

Tenants value basements because they can be used for storage, a home gym, or if it's in good shape—a family room. From the investor's perspective however, houses with basements have the potential for water leaks, and some investors avoid them and buy only houses built on a slab foundation.

In some markets like Kansas City, basements are a plus because that market has a tornado about once every ten years, and the residents are supposed to run to the basement when that happens. Having a basement in such a market could be a selling point in getting your property rented quickly.

The same is true for garages. They can be used for storage, for a home gym, or even to store a car or two and, unlike basements, don't really have a downside from the investor's perspective. Garages are better than car ports, but just having a dedicated parking spot is a plus for many tenants.

If the property you're considering has no garage, put yourself in the shoes of your tenant. Where would you store bikes, garbage bins, or tools? If the property offers no place for these items, your pool of tenants will likely be smaller.

Another consideration for two-car garages: Some homes have two small garage doors, and others have one big garage door (see photo).

Exhibit 8.1: Garage Door Types

Two small garage doors   **One large garage door**

Other things being equal, I prefer to have one big garage door. First of all, having one door instead of two means I'll get half the number of service calls about broken garage door openers! Secondly, in some markets like Houston, people drive monster pick-up trucks with fat tires and it's hard to drive them through one small garage door, but easy to get through a single, large garage door.

Does this mean you should never buy a house with two small garage doors? Not at all. If the property is a good property, the numbers work, and it's a good deal, then buy it. Someone will rent it and someone will buy it from you when you're ready to sell. It's just that in some markets, you might eliminate some potential renters right off the top.

Again, ask your property manager how big a deal this is in your market.

Two-Story vs. One-Story

Similar considerations apply to one-story vs. two-story homes.

In some Florida markets with lots of retirees, two-story homes are not popular because older people don't want to climb up and down the stairs. They may have a bad knee or a bad back and just don't want to deal with it. In an area with a large retirement population, you might lose a quarter of your potential renters by having a two-story home instead of a single story.

In other markets dominated by growing families, a two-story home might be preferred.

Ask your property manager for guidance about property types, features, and locations.

Pools

Are pools a good amenity for a rental property? Some investors say not to buy houses with pools because you can get sued if a little kid drowns. The cliché is "pools are for fools." Other investors will tell you that the landlord isn't legally responsible for what the tenants do.

That may be true, but in our litigious society, more and more lawsuits are being filed than ever. Even if the landlord isn't responsible, tenants with nothing to lose can still file a suit. Reflecting the added risk from pools, insurance rates will be $120-$150 per year higher for a property with a pool.

On the other hand, in some markets like Florida, pools are highly sought after by both tenants and your eventual buyers when you go to sell the property. You should discuss with your property manager whether she thinks pools are a good idea in your market.

If you're going to consider having a pool, here are some guidelines:

- Make sure the pool is less than ten years old so you don't have pool repair expenses.

- Have a pool screen/mosquito net around it so little kids can't easily access it.

- Have a property management addendum that states the landlord does not have an onsite lifeguarding service and is not responsible for what the tenant does or does not do.

- Have your property manager manage the pool maintenance and charge for it, usually about $75/month.

- Talk to your insurance agent to make sure you're adequately covered.

Trees

Trees are a desirable feature as they provide shade in the summertime, and many people like to barbeque outside during that time of year.

War Story

I had a client who owned a property in Cleveland and a large tree fell down during a storm and had to be cut down and removed. From that point on, the tenant experienced water seepage into the basement every time it rained. What they think happened was that the tree's root system was absorbing a lot of rainwater, and when the tree was removed the excess rain had nowhere to go and found its way into the basement. That's real estate—things happen! After sealing the basement, the investor planted two small trees to replace the one large tree, and there hasn't been a problem since.

Septic/Well

In some rapidly-growing metros, homes are being built faster than the local infrastructure, and many homes are built that do not have city sewer and water. In these areas, each home has a septic tank for waste and a well for water, somewhat like a mini-sewer/water system per house.

In newer homes—say built in 2000 or newer—these systems work fine and are not a reason to not invest in the properties that have them. For older homes, there are a few things to check before buying.

Let's discuss each in turn.

Septic

Modern septic systems can last thirty years and function well. There is a remote chance that in heavy rains, the septic's drain fields will become saturated, making it difficult for the septic's water to flow out of your drain system. In the event that happens, the septic system can back up. With modern systems, that happens only rarely.

The main downside to septic is that they have to be pumped and emptied out every few years, though at a modest cost of about $200. Many landlords put a clause in the lease stating that it's the tenant's responsibility to service the septic system—just as it is to pay the utility bills—and leave it up to the tenant to maintain the system. Personally, I would rather have my property management company do it on a periodic basis (every two years) and either charge it to the tenant or pay for it myself. I'd trust my property manager's maintenance schedule more than I'd trust a tenant to remember it.

While you're at it, ask the company that services the septic system for a copy of their maintenance records for the property. Look for repeated visits to fix problems.

Wells

There are several advantages to having well water instead of city-supplied water.

First, there are no water bills! This not only makes your tenant happy but may also save your lawn. If the tenant has to pay for water, there's a good chance she won't water the lawn frequently enough and, in the summer, your nicely landscaped lawn and backyard will wither.

The other advantage is that well water often tastes better because it doesn't have the city-treated chemical additives in it.

The downside is that the wells are often dug 100 feet or more into the ground, and the pumps that bring the water into your house will have to be replaced about every ten years. Again, this is an item I'd have on your property manager's maintenance schedule for the property.

For older homes but before 2000, there are some checks you should make before buying the home:

1. Confirm that it is a private well, not a well shared by two or more houses.

2. Confirm that the well and the septic system are at least 100 feet apart. Otherwise, if the septic tank backs up for some reason, it could potentially contaminate your water supply. Municipal building codes today require this distance, but older homes may not be in compliance.

3. If you want to be super-cautious, you can have the water tested both for quality (no E. coli or excessive minerals) and quantity (3-5 gallons per minute) by a licensed water inspector—above and beyond the standard home inspection. Finally, for both older and newer homes on well/septic, you should research whether or not the local municipality has plans to convert the neighborhood to city water/sewer.

Connecting to city water/sewer might cost you a one-time assessment of $20,000 or more and, while it might be a good long-term investment for your property, it can take a bite out of your capital in the short-term. Check with local city and county government websites and search for future utility connection projects.

Rehab Quality

If the property you're buying has been renovated, you have to pay special attention to the quality of the rehab. Some turnkey providers will put their rehab budget into cosmetics that look good to make the property sell quickly, but a few months later the hapless owner has major repairs like roof leaks or plumbing problems.

The turnkey provider should invest his budget into the "big ticket" items that could cost the investor lots of money down-the-road and deliver a solid, performing property. If there's any money left over in the budget, then that can be used for cosmetics like granite countertops and subway tile backsplashes.

The "big ticket" items are the following five: foundation, roof, electrical, plumbing, and HVAC.

If those items are in good shape, then you have yourself a good investment property. Here's what you should ask your property inspector to look out for:

Foundation

Check for cracks—not only in the foundation—but also in the walls, as that's an indicator that the ground has settled. Some markets like Dallas are notorious for having foundation issues, but the flip side is that they're very expert at fixing those problems.

Roof

The roof should have at least five years of useful life left on it. Ask when the roof was last replaced and if you're not sure, have it inspected by a roofer, not just the generic home inspector.

Electrical

Is the electrical up to current code, and do the bath outlets have GFCI (Ground Fault Circuit Interrupter)? If it's an older home, did they put multiple outlets in each room? In the '50s—before home computers, cell phones, and electric toothbrushes—some homes had only one outlet per room.

Plumbing

If the property is in a cold climate, have the old copper pipes been replaced with new PEX (polyethylene) pipes? PEX is typically more flexible than PVC; it can freeze and thaw without ever rupturing. Further, PEX is generally run in a single continuous line from source to fixture, so there are very few intermediate connections.

HVAC

Do the furnace and air conditioner work? Do they warm or cool all areas of the house? Is the furnace modern? Does the outside A/C unit have a cage so no one will steal it?

Other things to look for

This is by no means a comprehensive list, as that could be a topic for a whole other book, but a list of major items to consider when buying an investment property would include:

- Floor Plans

  Open floor plans are popular as of this writing

- Exterior Construction

  Brick exteriors last longer and require no maintenance as compared with siding.

- Flooring

  Luxury Vinyl Tile (LVT) or hardwood floors last longer than carpet, and carpet is expensive to replace every five to seven years. However, in colder climates, tenants won't rent a house that doesn't have carpet in the bedrooms, so you'll have to provide carpet. Ask your property manager what is needed in your market. Ideally you can keep LVT or hardwood floors in common areas and have carpet only in the bedrooms.

- Parking

  Garages are more desirable than car ports, car ports more desirable than driveways. Sometimes you'll find a garage that has been converted to a fourth bedroom, so there's a driveway but no garage.

Also, make sure the driveway is paved, and not dirt. When it rains, the dirt turns to mud. I once had to pay $1,000 to have gravel laid on a dirt driveway because the tenant's car was stuck in the mud and he couldn't drive to work.

Bottom line, when looking at the quality of the rehab, you have to ask yourself: Would this property attract a quality tenant who wants to live there and stay there?

STICKINESS

Turnover will kill your cash flow because you'll have a month of vacancy, make-ready costs, and leasing fee costs. You want to make this property "sticky" i.e., once someone moves in, they won't want to leave. Some ways to achieve that include:

- Rents just below the going rate

- Nicer touches vs. similarly priced rentals, such as lighting, laundry room, granite countertops, and fixtures. The tenant knows that, for the same rent, she won't be able to find anything comparable.

- Walking distance to public transportation, especially if in "C" neighborhoods.

- Walking distance to schools or daycare centers

- Responsive customer service. If the tenant has a problem with a leaky roof or broken garbage disposal, you have it fixed immediately. Your tenant is your customer and if you treat your customer right, she'll stick around longer.

VIRTUAL TOURS

In this day of global pandemics, scheduling walk-through inspections of a property is more of a challenge. Under normal conditions, you would fly to the city where you're investing, meet with the property manager, and conduct a walk-through of the property, then go to the title company and sign the documents.

As of this writing, many investors aren't comfortable getting on a plane, so 90% of transactions are done sight unseen.

This is accomplished through virtual tours and here's how they work.

The property manager or her leasing agent will take a video camera and walk through the property room-by-room and provide a detailed virtual walk-through of the property to give you, the investor, a good idea of what you're buying.

But any old walk-through won't suffice—here are three things to ask for specifically. Let's assume it's the leasing agent who will be doing the tour.

Detail

Instead of a whirlwind tour, the leasing agent should take the time to showcase the details of each room. I tell the agent to imagine the potential tenant is standing right beside her—how would you "sell" this property to them so they want to submit an application?

Kitchen: Show the countertops, a close-up of the fixtures (turn the water on and off), the cabinets (open and shut), the tiles used for flooring, and the appliances (open and shut).

Bathrooms: Show the tiles, close-ups of the fixtures, open the medicine cabinets and linen closet.

Other rooms: Show the bedroom carpets, open and close all closet doors to allow a peek inside, the ceiling fans, the windows (dual-paned or not?), and views from each window so you the investor have a good idea of what the house is like. Show the washer-dryer or the hookups.

Garage/Basements: Show the garage door in operation, show how clean the floor is and what space there is for storage.

Exterior: The video of the exterior should cover the entire property, 360 degrees. See if there are cracks in the foundation or walls, signs of water damage. Video the gutters and see that they have sufficient overhang so that rain won't run down the wall. All it takes is for a little crack in the wall and you'd have water damage.

Roof: A video of the roof should show a newer roof, with no shingles missing.

Landscaping: Show the lawn—both in the front and back of the house—the condition of the fencing, and the sprinkler system in operation if there is one.

AC Unit with Cage: The A/C unit is usually outside, and you want to see that it's modern and is covered by a cage, otherwise someone might steal it.

Water Heater: Water heaters have dates on them so you can see how old it is.

Furnace: Look for how new or worn the furnace is and compare that to the inspection report's estimate of useful life.

Neighborhood

When you're buying a house, you're also buying the neighborhood, so the video tour should give you a view up and down the street. Are the other houses well-maintained? Do the people have pride of ownership and mow their lawns and keep their driveways uncluttered? Are there nice cars in the neighborhood or clunkers? Are there power lines overhead near the property you're considering? Is the house on a busy street with lots of traffic noise? These are things you can't tell from Google Maps, so the video tour should answer these questions for you as much as possible.

Some questions can't be answered easily. As I mentioned in Chapter 6, when I visit a property—especially in a "C" neighborhood—I like to drive by on a weekend night to see if there are any domestic disturbances or even drug dealers. Good luck getting your leasing agent to do that.

Behind the house

This is something most people don't think to look for. What's behind the house? Who lives back there? Does the couple argue a lot? Do they have a bunch of barking dogs? Are there little kids in the yard screaming? Walking around the block to see who or what is on the other side of the house helps remove one more loose end.

In a way, the house itself is relatively easy because we, the investors, can control the house through the rehab quality.

The hard part is getting a handle on things you don't control (like the neighbors) and a complete due diligence process should include those things as well.

It's not uncommon for such a video tour to take 15-20 minutes, but it helps removes the FUD factor (Fear, Uncertainty, and Doubt) when you, the investor, are considering buying a property. A confused mind always says "no," so the leasing agent should do her best to make you comfortable making a such a large and illiquid investment without seeing it in-person.

CHAPTER 9
FINANCING

In this chapter, we'll discuss some considerations and potential pitfalls when deciding on financing.

ALL-CASH VS. FINANCED

The first decision you have to make is whether it's best to use financing at all, and in almost all cases, the answer is "yes." Financing—especially with interest rates as low as they are as of this writing—will enable you to achieve your financial goals faster.

For example, suppose you had $100,000 to invest and were considering investing in Memphis, TN, where investment properties cost about $100,000.

As the table below shows, with $100,000 to invest, you could buy one house all-cash, or about four houses with financing. The four houses with financing will yield more annual cash flow ($10,896) than the one house purchased all-cash ($7,860). Additionally, if the market appreciates, four houses appreciating will grow your equity more than one house appreciating.

Exhibit 9.1: Cash vs. Financed Scenario

123 Main St. Memphis TN	One House All-Cash	One House Financed	Four Houses Financed
Selling Price	100,000	100,000	400,000
Down Payment @ 20%	-	20,000	80,000
Closing Costs	1,500	3,000	12,000
All-in Acquisition Cost	*101,500*	*23,000*	*92,000*
Rent	1,000	1,000	4,000
Mortgage Payment @5.00%	-	428	1,712
Property Taxes	100	100	400
Insurance	65	65	260
Property Management @8.0%	80	80	320
Maintenance @5.0%	50	50	200
CapEx@ 5.0%	50	50	200
Total Expenses	*345*	*773*	*3,092*
Monthly Cash Flow	655	227	908
Annual Cash Flow	7,860	2,724	10,896
Cash-on-Cash Return	*7.7%*	*11.8%*	*11.8%*
(Annual Cash Flow/Acq Cost)			

The reason for the improved cash-on-cash returns with financing is due to positive leverage.

Note that, for the all-cash scenario, your return is 7.7% (i.e., you're making $7,860 in cash flow on an investment of $101,500, which comes to 7.7%). However, you're borrowing money at 5.0%.

Whenever you can borrow money at 5.0% and invest it in an asset yielding 7.7%, you're making a 2.7% "profit" just on the spread.

Imagine if you could borrow a billion dollars at 5.0% and invest it in something that yielded 7.7%. After one year, you'd make $27 million dollars—just on the spread between your borrowing cost and your return!

Real estate works the same way, only in addition to your return, you also get depreciation tax write-offs and potentially some appreciation in the property value as well. This is why it makes sense to borrow money when rates are low so you can finance multiple investment properties.

DOWN PAYMENT

As previously mentioned (but it bears repeating), when purchasing a property, you should ask your lender what the interest rate would be if you put 25% down (rather than 20%, as in the example above). Usually, you get a lower rate for 25% down, but after that it doesn't matter: You could put 25% down or 50% down and the rate would be the same. Usually there's a price break at 25%.

In general, the longer you hold the property, the more advantageous it is to pay a little more upfront and get the lower interest rate. As many investors wind up holding onto property longer than they originally intended, you may want to err on the side of putting more down payment and locking in the lower rate.

Check with your lender and get quotes for interest rates and monthly payments under both scenarios (20% down and 25% down) and see what the tradeoffs are. Typically, they'll send you a table like the one shown in Exhibit 9.2.

Exhibit 9.2: Loan Options

Rate	P & I	Points / Lender Credit ($/%)	LockPeriod/Days
3.625	$365	2.000% ($1600)	45
4.000	$382	1.750% ($1400)	45
4.125	$388	1.500% ($1200)	45
4.875	$423	1.250% ($1000)	45
5.000	$429	1.125% ($900)	45
5.125	$436	0.625% ($500)	45

How would you evaluate your options here? As an example, let's compare the difference between the highest and the lowest interest rates.

Difference in Principal and Interest (P&I) monthly payment = $436 - $365 = $71/month x 12 months = $852/year in savings at the lower rate. If you held the property for five years, that would be 5 x $852 in P&I savings, or $4,260.

On the other hand, the difference in points is only $1,600 - $500 = $1,100.

Would you be willing to pay an additional $1,100 now to save $4,260 over the next five years?

Or, if you held the property for ten years, to save $8,520?

Doing a cost-benefit analysis like this, the benefit ($4,260 in savings) outweighs the cost ($1,100). So consider how long you plan to hold the property, look at the various financing options, and do the math. Speaking for myself, I'd go for the lowest interest rate.

DEBT MAGNIFIES EVERYTHING

A word of caution about using debt: Debt magnifies everything. When times are good and real estate is booming, using debt to finance more properties will make you richer, quicker. But when times are bad and real estate is crashing, being leveraged to the hilt can make you bankrupt. *Debt magnifies everything.*

Debt is a tool. It increases your returns, but also increases your risk. A lot of investors got wiped out in the 2008-10 downturn because they were over-leveraged. Many used risky loans like adjustable-rate mortgages (ARMs) and interest-only loans. Some used Home Equity Lines of Credit (HELOCs) to finance their down payments and when their home values declined, the bank called the lines of credit due.

Make sure that with whatever level of debt you sign up for, the rental income can cover the mortgage payments and the investment is cash-flow positive. Do a sensitivity analysis on your investments:

- How much can vacancies go up and still leave you cash-flow positive? In the financed single-home example above, you could have two months of vacancy per year and still have positive cash flow of $724 per year ($2,724 - $2,000 in lost rents = $724).

- How much can rents go down and still leave you cash-flow positive? In the financed example above, rents could go down $200 per month and you'd still have positive $27 per month in cash flow.

FINDING LENDERS

You can get lender referrals from whomever you're buying the property, or through REIA and Meetup member recommendations. Regardless of how you find them, you should understand the different types of lenders available to you.

Direct lender vs. loan broker

A direct lender is a company that will lend you *their* money. It could be a bank or savings & loan that gets its capital from customer deposits, or it could be a mortgage lender that uses private capital.

A loan broker, on the other hand, is an intermediary who takes your loan application and "shops it around" to maybe a half dozen potential lenders to find the best lender and best rate for you. The downside is that he'll add his fee to your loan origination costs, and you have to consider whether the additional fee will negate the benefit of possibly finding a lower rate. Most lending today is highly competitive so rates should be comparable.

The other advantage of a loan broker is that he will save you time. If you were to shop around among various banks on your own, each bank would require you to submit a loan application, submit two years' worth of tax returns, two years' worth of W-2 statements, the last two months of bank statements for each bank you do business with, and other documents. This is time-consuming. With a loan broker, you submit these documents once to the broker and he takes it from there.

Also, each bank will run a credit report on you with each of the three credit reporting agencies (Equifax, Experian, and TransUnion); having multiple requests for your credit report will raise a red flag (unjustifiably in this case) and cause you to lose a few points on your credit score. With a loan broker, your credit score is run once.

That said, each credit report run might deduct five points from your FICO score, and since the range of scores is 300 – 850, only the most marginal buyers should be affected. If your score is 790 or higher, having your credit run every three months or so should have little effect on your score.

National vs. local lender

National companies like Wells Fargo, Bank of America, JPMorgan Chase, Citibank, et al., can lend nationwide, but can also be very bureaucratic and harder to work with. For example, a Florida turnkey provider I know will not work with a certain national bank because the process involves dealing with multiple loan officers in different offices around the country, depending on where the loan application is in the process. That bank sometimes takes two months to approve a loan!

At the other end of the spectrum, a local lender could be a regional bank like Regions Bank in the Southeast, or PNC Bank in the Northeast, or a savings & loan. In general, these companies usually have better knowledge of local markets and a more streamlined process but may not lend in all states where you want to invest.

If your investment plan is to eventually own multiple properties in multiple regions around the country, it might be handier to have your paperwork on file in one place and be able to borrow anywhere. Everything's a tradeoff.

Banks vs. online lenders

The latest entry into the field are online lenders like Rocket Mortgage by Quicken Loans.

Possible advantages of an online lender are that they can approve or deny your loan application very quickly and can often be more lenient if you have a lower credit score, a foreclosure, or a bankruptcy in your history. This is because they're not banks and therefore do not have to comply with a myriad of federal lending and reporting compliance laws.

The disadvantages are that they usually do not have a physical retail location where you can walk in and meet with someone face-to-face—which is especially helpful for a first-time investor. If you call the customer service 800#, you'll likely get a different person each time and have to explain your situation repeatedly.

A second consideration is that an online lender will usually sell your loan to a loan servicing company after close. That means that you will have little to no say in which financial institution you make your monthly mortgage payments to.

Note: The selling of your loan can also happen with a conventional bank.

Conventional vs. non-conventional

Another way to slice-and-dice the lending world is to look at conventional vs. non-conventional lenders.

A conventional lender gives loans backed by Fannie Mae or Freddie Mac, two government-sponsored enterprises that make mortgages available by borrowing in the debt markets using those funds to purchase loans from loan originators, like banks, S&Ls, etc. They do not provide loans themselves, but back or guarantee them in the secondary mortgage market.

You as an investor can have as many as ten conventional Fannie/Freddie loans. If you have a working spouse, I always recommend you put ten houses in your name and ten houses in your spouse's name, for a household total of twenty. I've seen investors make the mistake of having both spouses on each loan, which means as a couple you'll max out at ten loans instead of twenty.

If you and your spouse are both on the loan for your primary residence, then that leaves nine loans available to each of you for investment properties.

Note: FHA loans and VA loans are only applicable to owner-occupants, i.e. borrowers who are buying a house to live in, not buying as an investment to rent to tenants.

A non-conventional lender lends to investors without the guarantees of Fannie and Freddie. As a result, the interest rate they charge could be a full percentage point or more higher than a conventional Fannie/Freddie loan, and may require a higher down payment.

These loans are useful in certain situations. For example, if you are maxed out on your Fannie/Freddie loans and want to buy more properties, you need to work with a non-conventional lender to get loan number eleven and beyond.

Extra for Experts: Using IRA money to finance investment property

For some investors, money saved in their Individual Retirement Accounts (IRAs) is a tempting source of money to buy more investment properties. While doable, in my view this should be done only as a last resort.

Your IRA is a tax-deferred account and, as such, using IRA money as a source of capital will make you lose some of the benefits of real estate investing. You can't write off interest on your loans and you can't take depreciation write-offs on your property. Since you're not paying taxes on any gains, you can't take tax write-offs on your expenses either. Now if you run the numbers and decide that the investment is sound even if it means losing those benefits, or if using IRA funds is the only way you can invest, then IRA money may be an option for you.

You can either buy all-cash—which is simplest—or use your IRA money for the down payment and get a non-recourse loan to finance the rest. A non-recourse loan is one that uses the financed property and only the financed property as collateral. If you default, the lender can foreclose and take possession of the property, but not take possession of your other assets like your bank account or primary residence. This is because tax law considers your IRA to be a separate entity, meaning that you're not borrowing the money, your IRA is. As a result, the non-recourse lender can't come after you personally to pay the loan, only your IRA.

The non-recourse lender will require a higher down payment (around 30%) and charge a higher interest rate (usually one or two percentage points higher than the going market rate). These are reasons why you should use IRA money only if you have no other source of capital for your down payment.

Personally, I use IRA money to invest in the stock market and non-IRA money for direct ownership of real estate, and that works out pretty well.

Bottom line: For most investors, the best approach is to get as many conventional Fannie/Freddie loans as possible, as these types of loans have lower interest rates and lower down payment requirements, which make for better investor returns. They're also more lender-friendly because the lender's risk is mitigated by being guaranteed by quasi-government agencies.

When you've exhausted all your conventional loans, then it's time to start looking for non-conventional options.

CHAPTER 10

BUYING

APPRAISAL AND INSPECTIONS

As part of the purchase process, you will need an appraisal and one or more inspections.

Appraisal

Performed by a state-licensed appraiser, the appraisal is the official estimate for how much the property is worth, based on comparable sales of properties in the same area, the condition of the home, and other factors. It usually costs $300-$400, depending on the size of the home and what the local going rate is.

Note: An appraisal is not to be confused with a "Broker Price Opinion" (BPO), which is basically a short-cut appraisal. In a BPO, a licensed real estate broker will look up comparable sales online and then do a drive-by of the property and make an educated guess as to its current market value.

The key difference between the two is that in an appraisal, the appraiser goes inside the home and examines its condition. Are the carpets new or worn? Are there nice granite countertops or Formica? Are the bathroom tiles modern or some hideous green color from the 1960s? A drive-by of the exterior of the home cannot capture these essential items.

What if it doesn't appraise? Let's say the selling price is $150,000 but the appraiser says it's worth only $140,000. In that case, you should negotiate the price down to $140,000. After all, the bank won't lend on the property above its appraised value. If you're really in love with the house, you might split the difference with the seller—e.g., you put an additional $5,000 into the down payment and the seller comes down in price by $5,000.

Inspections

Similarly, an inspection is conducted by a state-licensed property inspector; it tells you the current condition of the property. Is the electrical system up to code? Are the sewage pipes rusted or cracked? Do all the electrical outlets and faucets work? Does the roof leak? Are there cracks in the foundation? The inspector provides a "clean bill of health" for the property—or itemizes what's not up to snuff. This costs about $300-$400 on average, and as little as $200 if it's for a condominium unit.

Almost all inspections find something wrong with the property—that's how they justify their fees, so you have to take that into account when negotiating with the seller to fix certain items. Inspection findings should be broken down into categories, ranked by seriousness:

- Items that are safety hazards such as exposed electrical wiring, or staircases without handrails.

- Structural defects such as cracks in the walls or foundation, rusted pipes, leaky roofs or basements, drafty windows, non-functioning garbage disposal, and the like.

- Cosmetic defects such as mismatched paint, discolored tiles or roof shingles, holes in interior doors or walls, cracks in the bathroom mirror, etc.

The "big five" items are the ones that can cost you a lot of money to repair later, so your inspector should focus on them: foundation, roof, electrical, plumbing, and HVAC (heating, ventilation, and air conditioning). If those are in good shape, you shouldn't have any major expenses.

Not all inspectors do a thorough job and not all itemize their findings. You should either specify that you want the findings broken down by the three categories bulleted above or ask to see a copy of a past inspection report so you know what to expect.

War Story

I once saw an inspection report with comments like "The electrical outlets all appear to work...".

What does that mean?? Did the inspector check each outlet, or didn't he? If he cut corners here, where else did he cut corners? Getting a sample copy of a past report will help you avoid unpleasant surprises later.

FOLLOW-UP INSPECTIONS

Sometimes the inspector will identify potential issues and recommend that it be investigated by a specialist. In each of the following examples, make sure the inspector provides not only an inspection report but also an estimate of how much it would cost to remediate any issues.

Wood-destroying organisms (WDO) inspection

This additional inspection may be something your inspector recommended, or in a humid climate like Louisiana it might be required by your lender. This inspection checks for termites and wood rot on the exterior siding, interior walls and baseboards, and the garage. The inspection report should tell you how serious any wood rot is, and what the cost would be to remediate it.

Mold

Mold is another health hazard and should be remediated if discovered by the initial inspection. Make sure the mold inspector reports not only on the mold, but also what caused it. If it was the result of leaky pipes causing moisture to build up somewhere in the property, then you'd want to address the leaky pipes too, or the mold will simply return. Also, make sure the mold inspector has no conflict of interest: Some will say there's mold so they can get hired to be the one to remediate it. Make it clear that they're there to do the inspection only.

Lead-based paint inspection

Lead paint is a health hazard and is common in properties built before 1978. The seller is required to disclose any knowledge of lead paint in the Seller Disclosure Form. Generally, you wouldn't order a lead inspection unless the first inspection identified it as an issue and recommended a lead-specific inspection. I personally have never seen one done. In many markets, having a property flagged as having a lead paint issue will make it difficult to sell, so I would avoid having a lead inspection done if possible.

If there is lead-based paint, removing it is done either by wire brushing, hand-scraping with paint removers, or an electric sander equipped with a high-efficiency particulate air (HEPA) filtered vacuum. These measures can add significant expense to your property to make it suitable for habitation.

Sewer inspections

In homes built in the 1950s or earlier, you should consider getting an additional sewer inspection—i.e., the sewer line between the house and the main sewer line in the street. A property inspection only covers the property itself—it does not include the sewer line from the house to the main sewer line in the street. If your sewer cracks and needs to be replaced, it can cost up to $4,000. The contractor will have to tear up the street, dig down to the sewer line, replace it, and then re-cover and re-pave the street. I had to do this with one of my houses in Kansas City years ago.

Another option is to get a sewer insurance policy for about $10 per month after you purchase the home, and that policy will cover the expense of repairing the sewer line in the event you have a problem. This can save you the $300 to have a sewer inspection done on a property that you aren't yet sure you're going to buy yet.

Radon gas

Radon is a radioactive gas that is present in homes all over the United States and is most commonly found in houses with basements. Long-term exposure to radon gas has proven to contribute to lung cancer deaths every year. For a map of which parts of the US are more prone to having radon problems, visit the EPA site at https://www.epa.gov/radon/epa-map-radon-zones.

The good news is that most licensed home inspectors are also able to check for radon (for an additional fee) when doing the initial inspection. If your property has a basement and/or is located in one of the areas prone to have radon issues, I recommend you have it done, just for peace of mind. When choosing a home inspector, find out if he's able to do a radon inspection at the same time he's doing the general inspection.

Defective Chinese drywall

A lesser-known inspection is one that tests for defective Chinese drywall, manufactured and installed in 2001-2009, which was not made to US specifications. That drywall has high levels of sulfur, which results in a "rotten egg" smell in the house, blackened pipes, breakdown of air conditioners, and health problems such as asthma, coughing, headaches, and sore eyes.

War Story

An investing buddy of mine bought three investment properties in Houston, in which the home builder had sourced drywall from China to save on costs—drywall is drywall, right? His tenants had to evacuate the properties, all the walls had to be ripped out, replaced, and re-painted. He eventually sold all three properties at a loss.

The Chinese drywall issue affected only 100,000 homes in about twenty states, so the odds of running into this is small, but you should be aware of it.

FINDING APPRAISERS AND INSPECTORS

Often, the seller or real estate agent will offer you a list of appraisers and inspectors they've worked with in the past, but that can be risky. How do you know that appraiser isn't the seller's brother-in-law? You want to be certain that you're getting an unbiased appraisal. The same applies to any property inspectors they recommend. Yes, if it turns out they are biasing their reports in favor of the seller they can lose their license, but that's very hard to prove.

How to protect yourself: Ask your lender to recommend appraisers and inspectors. Your bank has a vested interest in making sure the appraisal and inspection are accurate, because the bank is using the property as collateral for the loan. If you can find an appraiser or an inspector who is on both the lender's list and the seller's list, then you have the best of both worlds.

War Story

Using the bank's recommended appraiser has some risks too. Usually, the bank has a database of vendors and when they need one, their software will pick the cheapest vendor who's available at the time. The "lowest bidder" may not be the most competent vendor.

Some appraisers and inspectors will claim expertise in neighborhoods they know little about, because they want to get more bids. And when they do have to appraise a property out of their area of competence and experience, they'll often be conservative and err on the low side. If that house you were planning to buy for $100,000 appraises for only $90,000, the bank may not finance it and you'll lose the deal.

Like anything else in investing, there's a balancing act. Most of the time, the bank's appraisers and inspectors will be fine, but you should be aware of this potential pitfall.

Tip

Make sure that all utilities are turned on before scheduling the appraisals and inspections. If the electricity is off, the inspector can't tell if the lights or appliances work and may not even be able to see areas like the basement very well. Then you'll have to pay for a second inspection. This happens surprisingly often, especially with new-construction homes.

Also, if the property has a tenant already in it, it's better to schedule the inspection and the appraisal on the same day, to avoid inconveniencing the tenant more than necessary.

Statement of work

If the inspection identifies areas that need correction, make sure all work is completed before closing, not after. Once you've closed, you no longer have any leverage with the seller. You're low priority because the seller already has your money. If you're under a deadline—such as a 1031 exchange—and renovations are not finished, include a "completed-by" date in the sales contract.

War Story

I had a client who purchased a home in January 2018 that was supposed to be renovated within six months, and as of April 2019, the work hadn't even begun! For any purchase involving renovations after the close of escrow, include a statement of work (SOW) and a "completed-by" date in the sales contract.

Buyer's Walk-Through Inspection

If possible, you should visit the property in-person and do a walk-through with the leasing agent or property manager.

You should bring a copy of the initial inspection report and its "punch list" of items needing repair so you can confirm that they have, in fact, been repaired. Don't assume anything! I've had property management companies tell me that inspection items had been taken care of and, upon re-inspection, it was obvious they had not! This is a classic case of the property manager's office not knowing what their field crews were doing. This happens surprisingly frequently.

As mentioned earlier, if an in-person walk-through is not possible, you can always ask for a "virtual tour" by video. In that case, I would make sure the person filming the tour has a copy of the inspection report and you've instructed her to show in the video that each repair has been made.

As you walk-through or watch the video, think not only as the future owner but also as a future tenant: Would you as a tenant want to live here? What kind of tenant would be happy living here? This is your last chance to discuss improvements with your property manager.

Contract Contingencies

Your purchase contract should contain a few contingencies so you can back out of the deal if something goes sideways. Following are three contingencies you should have for any investment property.

First, the sale should be contingent on the property appraising for the sale price. If the price is $100,000 and the appraiser says it's worth $95,000, then the bank may not extend the loan and you should be able to back out of the deal. Or you can negotiate a lower price with the seller.

For an investment property, when the numbers are so close, the parties usually split the difference, e.g., the seller comes down in price by $2,500 and the buyer adds $2,500 to the down payment.

The second contingency is for the inspection. If the inspection reveals serious problems that will be costly or time-consuming to repair, you want to be able to back out of the deal. The seller will include a "Seller Disclosure" form, noting all known issues with the house. Many will be minor, like a crack in the garage floor. But you should read the seller disclosure documents carefully and beware of "I don't know" answers. Hand the Seller Disclosure form to the licensed inspector and ask him to specifically look out for the items noted (how serious are they?) and the "I don't know" items ("Is there lead paint?") so you can find out if there's an issue.

The first two contingencies are ones you'd want to have for any home purchase, investment or primary residence. The third contingency is especially important for any out-of-town property you're considering buying: A walk-through inspection by the buyer.

If a property looks like it'll make a good investment, and you've done as much due diligence as you can online and you buy it, the time will come when you'll visit the property and see it in-person for the first time. That's why the sales contract should include "Contingent on a Walk-Through Inspection by the Buyer." If, for whatever reason, you don't like it, you have an escape clause and can get out.

Maybe it's on a noisy street with lots of traffic and you think it'll be hard to find a tenant. Maybe the neighbor next door has pit bulls that bark all day. These are things you won't see from Google Maps. If you don't have this escape clause, you won't be able to easily get out of the purchase.

Caveat: In hot markets, properties sell quickly, and you may not have time to fly out and see it before you purchase, so you need to have the ability to buy sight unseen while giving yourself an "out." Also, the seller may not agree to the walk-through contingency because the market is hot and he can find other buyers. You then have to balance your risk tolerance vs. what's realistic given market conditions. Your agent or turnkey provider should be able to make recommendations about your best course of action.

NEGOTIATIONS

In a seller's market, in which there are more buyers than properties available and there are multiple offers on each available property, you will not have much of a bargaining position to negotiate price.

But seller's markets are not the time to be buying anyway: As an investor, you should be buying when it's a buyer's market (many properties to choose from, desperate sellers), hold the property for a length of time, and then sell when it's a seller's market. (If you do nothing else in real estate investing, that strategy alone could help make you a successful investor!)

In a buyer's market, you will probably have enough bargaining power to negotiate the price or the terms of the property. Most investors try to negotiate the price, but even if you don't, you may want to negotiate closing costs instead. Consider the following example.

Let's say you twist the seller's arm and he comes down $4,000 in price. With 25% down, that saves you $1,000 out-of-pocket. On the other hand, if you can negotiate a $4,000 reduction in closing costs, that saves you $4,000 out-of-pocket. Even if you negotiate only a $2,000 reduction in closing costs, that will preserve more of your precious out-of-pocket capital than a $4,000 reduction in price.

You can only wheel-and-deal so much on any given property, so choose carefully which battles you want to fight.

HOMEOWNERS ASSOCIATIONS (HOAS)

Though covered in more detail in Chapter 13 (Condos), some new single-family subdivisions have HOAs, so it's worth touching on here. If your property is in a subdivision with an HOA, make sure you review the HOA's Covenants, Conditions, and Restrictions (CC&Rs) for the property and make sure they're not too onerous. Research the association online and see if they have a reputation for being unreasonably strict or difficult to work with. You as the owner are responsible for any tenant violations, so you could be cited or fined.

At this point, the main concern is to make sure that there are no restrictions on your ability to rent the property. Some HOAs impose limits on what percent of a development can be rentals, or that you have to own the property for a year before being able to rent it. Check to see that there's nothing in the HOA that limits your ability to rent.

Also, make sure your tenants get a copy of the CC&Rs and include abiding by them in the lease agreement. If there's an infraction of HOA rules, the tenant will not be able to claim ignorance.

INSURANCE

Insuring an investment property is not the same as insuring a primary residence, so let's review the various types of insurance you need as an investor.

Title insurance

Title insurance protects both the property buyer and mortgage lender against problems relating to ownership. The most common claims filed against a title are back taxes, liens, and conflicting ownership.

If the previous owner owed back taxes on the property, that will show up in the title search. If the previous owner had work done on the house and didn't pay the contractors, a lien on the property will show up on the title search.

There may also be conflicting claims on who owns the property and therefore who is entitled to sell it. A common example is if the property is held in the name of a divorced couple and the seller didn't get the consent of his spouse before selling the property. Other examples of title problems include omissions in deeds, undisclosed heirs, forgery, or mistakes in records.

Performing a title search before final purchase of a property is therefore essential to ensure you will receive the title free and clear of any defects in ownership, and you won't be liable for any back taxes or liens. If an issue surfaces after close, the title insurance will pay for it.

Note that there are two kinds of title policies: A buyer's policy and a lender's policy. Your bank will require the lender's policy because that protects the lender in the event that a title issue arises in the future. The bank generally does NOT require that you, the buyer, have a buyer's policy, but you should get one anyway to protect yourself. The lender doesn't care if you're covered; the lender only cares if the lender is covered.

Here's an example: You buy an investment property in Ohio for $100,000 with 20% down. The lender will require a lender's policy of $80,000 (the amount of money the lender has at risk) to protect itself. But you, as the buyer, should also get a buyer's policy of $100,000 to protect yourself as well.

Dwelling insurance for landlords

Dwelling insurance is the type of policy you'll need for rental properties. Dwelling policies provide coverage for damage to your property from such losses as fire, wind, theft, vandalism, water damage, hail, and tornados. The policy provides coverage for the structure itself and built-in/attached appliances. Coverage may also include structures adjacent to the house, such as an attached garage, deck, or porch. Most policies provide 10% of the dwelling limit for detached "other structures" such as a detached garage.

How much insurance do you need? The insurance agent might try to sell you an expensive policy that covers everything and has small deductibles. A good rule of thumb is to protect yourself against expenses that would wipe you out financially. A kitchen fire may cause $5,000 in damage—that you can handle and don't need to insure for. On the other hand, if the entire house burns down, you can't handle that by yourself, so you'd want to insure yourself for that scenario.

Talk to your insurance agent about what level of coverage you need, and balance that against what you could cover out-of-pocket vs. what you need the insurance company to cover.

Empty or vacant property insurance

This insurance is useful to real estate investors who "flip" houses or any investor who has a vacant property on the rental market. A vacant house with a "For Rent" sign outside is a tempting target to thieves who'll break in and steal your appliances, your water heater—even your copper piping, not to mention the damage they can cause, like broken windows, kicked-in doors, etc. Make sure the vacant-property policy provides coverage for theft.

War Story

I had a vacant house in Kansas City years ago that was broken into. The vandals did about $3,000 worth of damage to the HVAC system—just to steal about a hundred dollars' worth of copper pipes. The next time I have a vacant home in a "C" neighborhood, I'll leave some copper pipes in a box with a sign saying, "Steal this and leave the plumbing alone!"

Tip

When you're trying to fill a vacancy, do not post the property address online, as it can attract thieves. Just post the general location ("near 5th and Main St") and provide the phone number of your leasing agent to answer any inquiries.

Vacant property insurance is especially important if you expect a lengthy vacancy—e.g., over the holidays when few people are moving. Consider also shutting the water valve while the property is vacant, in the unlikely event of a leak or burst pipe.

Homeowner's insurance

Homeowner's insurance is the policy you need for your primary residence—not your investment properties—so it's not relevant to this book. If you want to know more, any insurance agent will be happy to talk your ear off about it!

Renter's insurance

Renter's insurance (also known as "tenant insurance") is a policy your tenant may want to take out to protect their personal belongings from losses due to fire or burglary.

Unlike a homeowner's policy, it does not cover the building (that's the owner's responsibility) but only personal property like the tenant's clothes, furniture, and electronics. It may not cover items such as jewelry, guns, or a coin collection unless the tenant specifically adds those to the policy. A standard policy costs about $20 per month, so it's a modest expense for the tenant.

Some landlords require proof of renter's insurance as part of the lease agreement as a way of protecting themselves. Consider these issues:

- If damage occurs to a renter's belongings due to a fire, and the tenant does not have renter's insurance, there's a good chance he'll try to claim the landlord is responsible. If he has rental insurance, then he can pursue a claim with his insurance company.

- If the tenant is required by the lease to carry renter's insurance, and it can be demonstrated that the tenant caused the fire or loss, then the tenant's renter's policy would be liable to cover your losses.

- If fire damage causes the tenant to move into a hotel, tenant insurance can cover the hotel bill so the landlord is "off the hook" for providing accommodations.

Renter's insurance can also be a red flag. If your tenant can't pay $20-per-month, are they financially viable enough to be your tenant? If renter's insurance in one neighborhood is $50 whereas insurance in most neighborhoods is $20, you might question whether you want to buy property in that neighborhood.

Ask your property manager about renter's insurance and see what she recommends.

Umbrella insurance

Umbrella insurance is a form of liability insurance designed to protect you and your assets from damages arising from a lawsuit. While this possibility is "top of mind" for many investors, in reality it doesn't happen that often. First, you have to get sued, and secondly, the plaintiff has to win the judgment against you.

War Story

I know an investor with over 200 properties who's been investing for forty years and he's been sued only twice—and he won both cases. I know another investor who's been investing for twenty-five years and has never been sued.

That said, an umbrella policy can give you peace-of-mind for a modest expense, such as $200 per year for a $1,000,000 policy. This umbrella policy can be a lifesaver if you are found liable and need to pay damages, or even if you're not found liable but still incur legal expenses.

In either case, you the policy holder will have to pay only the deductible and, after that, the insurance company pays the rest up to the amount of your coverage. For example, let's say there's ice on your property's steps, someone slips and breaks a leg, and you get sued for $100,000 and are found liable. You will have to pay only your deductible of $10,000 and the insurance company pays the rest.

Note: Insurance is an important subject, and this overview is necessarily brief. Consult with your insurance agent to get a fuller explanation of your specific needs.

ENTITIES

On the subject of umbrella insurance, one investor question is whether to purchase their properties through an LLC (Limited Liability Company). LLCs are used by real estate investors to protect themselves (somewhat) from lawsuits. If an umbrella policy can provide protection against lawsuits, why get an LLC? This is another complicated subject, and you should consult with your attorney to determine what's best for you. But here are some guidelines:

Pros:

An LLC can give you some level of protection from lawsuits in that the LLC (not you) is the property owner. In the event of a lawsuit and a judgment against you, your liability is limited to the assets owned by the LLC. They can't take your primary residence, your car, your IRA, or 401(k).

If set up properly, an LLC can give you anonymity. No attorney will be able to do a search to find out what assets you own in order to decide whether to file a frivolous lawsuit against you. If they don't think you have anything, they'll look for someone else to sue.

Cons:

An investor can spend thousands of dollars setting up complicated structures like a Florida LLC with three properties that are "owned" by a Wyoming LLC. In addition to the setup costs, some states charge an annual maintenance fee to keep the LLC active.

If the investor doesn't maintain correct documentation and processes (e.g., record minutes of an annual meeting), the LLC could be disallowed anyway.

Some banks want the property and the loan in the name of the investor, not an LLC. Transferring legal ownership from the investor to the LLC could theoretically enable the lender to call the note due in full, though this happens rarely if at all.

War Story

California charges an annual fee of $800 per year per LLC—even if the LLC is registered in a different state! In the previous example, a California investor who owns three homes in her Florida LLC, which in turn is owned by a Wyoming LLC, has to pay California $1,600 per year. That would eat up much of the cash flow generated by those properties. Investors who live in California therefore tend to rely more on umbrella insurance policies for protection.

Dogma Alert!

I've seen many beginning investors spend lots of money on legal fees for complicated entity structures; money that could be spent buying more properties. I personally prefer to put my money in more properties—not legal fees—but you should consult with your attorney to see what's right for you.

HOW BUYERS AND SELLERS MISCOMMUNICATE

Finally, I'd like to discuss miscommunications that happen all too often in this industry. People with different frames of reference or from different parts of the country can use the same words but mean totally different things.

For example, a real estate agent in Kansas City once told me that in addition to the cash flow, a certain property could give me some appreciation, and that didn't make sense to me. It turns out his idea of "appreciation" was that a house purchased for $90,000 would be worth $100,000 ten years later. I've spent most of my working life in the San Francisco Bay Area, and when we say "appreciation" we mean a property that goes up by $100,000 or more—in one year!

The realtor wasn't trying to be deceptive. In his world, that's what "appreciation" means. But when dealing with someone from outside his area, he inadvertently miscommunicated.

Tip

To be unambiguous, avoid adjectives and replace them with numbers. Instead of asking "Is this an appreciating market?" ask "Is this market appreciating 10% per year or more?" or "What is the annual home price appreciation for existing homes?" Using specific numbers ensures that your and the seller's definitions of appreciation are on the same page.

Similarly, some real estate agents will quote statistics they don't quite understand. They may cite data from the MLS that shows "prices in this market have gone up X% in the last year," but this is often misleading. Consider the hypothetical market shown below.

Exhibit 10.1: How Statistics Can Mislead

	Last Year	This Year
Existing Homes		
- Sold	10	10
- Selling Price	$100K	$100K
New-Construction Homes		
- Sold	-	10
- Selling Price	-	$200K
Average Market Sales Price	*$100K*	*$150K*

In this simplified example, it is NOT accurate to say that "this market is appreciating 50% per year." The only reason the average MLS sales price went up 50% is because a bunch of new homes hit the market and skewed the averages. If you're buying one of the existing $100K homes in that market, you should expect flat appreciation, not 50%.

The real estate agent isn't necessarily trying to be deceptive. She just read a statistic somewhere, accepted it at face value, and used it as a selling point. When looking at statistics, always look "under the hood" and make sure you're comparing apples to apples.

Now that we've discussed buying, now let's look at the due diligence steps you should take when you decide to sell your property.

CHAPTER 11

SELLING

In this chapter, we'll discuss some considerations about how and when to sell your property. There are several exit strategies for an investment property, and you should have identified which one you're planning to use even before you originally purchased the property.

BUY-AND-HOLD INVESTING

Some investors are "buy-and-hold" investors. Their plan is to buy a house, never sell it, and let the tenants pay off the mortgage for them. Eventually, such investors will own a portfolio of properties free and clear, and they can live off the positive cash flow those properties generate.

The advantages of this approach are that the investor avoids all the transaction costs from selling.

Real estate is not as liquid as stocks or bonds, and selling involves (a) not renewing a tenant's lease; (b) waiting for them to leave; (c) paying for a make-ready to get the house ready for sale; (d) putting the house on the market; and (e) selling it. Aside from the hassle and all the work involved, the sale usually involves one to three months of vacancy depending on how fast the property sells, and also closing costs. By buying-and-holding, the investor avoids all that.

The potential downside to this approach is that as houses age, their maintenance costs go up. If you're thinking of a buy-and-hold strategy, the Key Performance Indicator (KPI) to watch is: Are expenses growing faster than rents? If your rents are going up 2.5% per year, e.g. from $1,000 per month to $1,025 per month, but your expenses are growing 5% per year, then sooner or later your cash flow will be squeezed. If you track your expenses every year and start to see that the expenses are growing faster than rents, it's time to consider selling the property if cash flow is your reason for owning the property.

That, by the way, is one of the issues with condos and Homeowners Association (HOA) dues. As the complex gets older, the HOA dues grow faster than rents, and your cash flow will get squeezed. See Chapter 13 for more detail.

On the other hand, if your goal is appreciation and not cash flow, you might want to hold on to the property. In the previous example, if the property is appreciating 10% per year, then it might make sense to keep it even if expenses are growing faster than rents. The gain from the appreciation will offset the squeeze on your cash flow. In general, holding makes sense while the market is appreciating.

WHEN TO SELL

A good rule of thumb for market timing (mentioned earlier) is to buy when it's a buyer's market and sell when it's a seller's market. Let's drill down on that a little further.

Markets don't appreciate forever. They go up and up but eventually prices are so high that most people in the area can't afford to buy them, so prices plateau and may even decline.

Typically, a home buyer can afford a property that's three times their annual gross income—e.g. if household income is $50,000, then that person can get a loan for a $150,000 house. If your property is in a zip code where the average household income is $50,000, you know prices are unlikely to go much above $150,000. If you bought the property for $100,000 and now comps show it's worth about $140,000, it might be time to get out of that market and sell.

A mistake many investors make in such a scenario is to try to hold on until the last minute and squeeze as much capital gain as possible from the property by selling at the exact peak of the market.

Consider the following graph from Zillow:

Exhibit 11.1: San Jose Average Home Price by Year

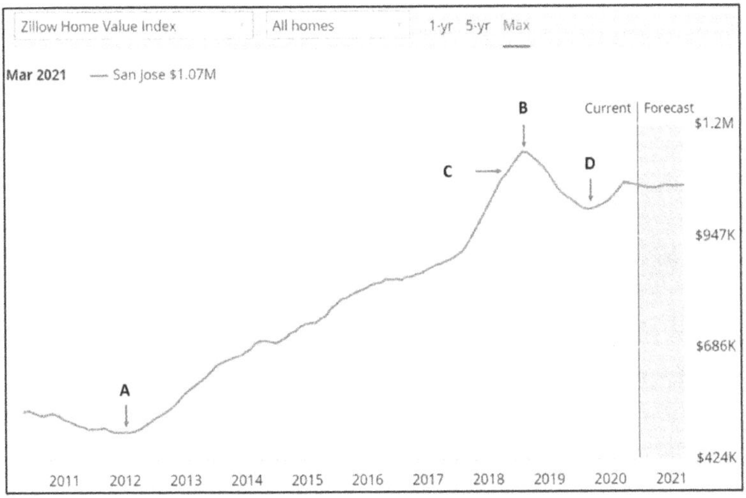

Here we see a graph showing the average home price in San Jose, CA, for a ten-year period. Note how (relatively) low the prices were after the Great Financial Crisis of 2008-10 and how much they've recovered.

What everyone wants to do is buy at Point A (the absolute bottom) and sell at Point B (the absolute top). This is unrealistic and risky, and here's why: You won't know where the absolute top is until after you've passed it. And after you've passed it, the buyer's psychology has changed.

As prices are rising (left of Point B) the buyer is panicky. She's made several offers, gotten into multiple bidding wars, and lost to higher bidders. Time is not on her side, and to get a home she knows she needs to pay above market because the longer she waits, the less likely it is that she'll be able to get a home.

But once prices start to soften, days on market start to increase, multiple offers start to decrease, then the buyer's mindset changes. Now she's thinking that time is now on her side, and maybe she can get a better deal if she waits a few months to see what happens. By the time you, the seller, actually sell the property, the price is more likely to be at Point D.

In this situation, I advise my clients to sell at Point C. Prices are still rising, homes are flying off the shelf, so get out while the getting's good.

This is something I learned from the stock market. If I bought a stock at $60 and it's gone up and just hit $92, I know what everyone else is thinking: "I'll wait until it hits $100 and then I'll sell." If it does hit $100, I know there's going to be a stampede for the exits, so I place my sell order at $95. Let someone else have the last few points—I'm getting out before the stampede.

This is even truer for real estate because real estate is not a highly liquid asset. If I time the stock market incorrectly, I can always go online 24/7 and liquidate my position and cut my losses. With real estate, if I missed the boat, it might be five or ten years before another good selling opportunity presents itself.

Look again at Exhibit 11.1. From Point A to Point C, the risk-reward ratio was in your favor, as the housing market was recovering from the Great Financial Crisis and the wind was at your back. From Point C to Point B, the risk-reward ratio is off-the-charts crazy. You had a good run, but you're greedy and want to hold out for the very top. Your risk is very high for a potential gain that is relatively low.

From Point A to Point C, you were an investor. From Point C to Point B, you become a speculator. Let the buyer have the last few points and get out.

WHO TO SELL TO

An investment property typically has three potential buyers: Your tenant, another investor, or an owner-occupant who's going to make the property his or her home. Each has pros and cons.

Selling to your tenant is the easiest option. Your tenant knows the property better than anyone else and selling to him doesn't require you give him notice, wait for him to leave, and then spend money to get the property ready for sale. You may not get top dollar by going this route, but the savings in time and money make this an attractive option.

Selling to another investor is also pretty easy, and the fact that the property already has a tenant with a proven track record makes it more desirable for another investor. Again, you may not get top dollar because the investor is looking at the property solely in terms of dollars and will try to drive a hard bargain.

An owner-occupant, on the other hand, plans to make the property her home so it's somewhat of an emotional decision. If she likes the house and the school district, she'll pay market rate or even above market rate to get the house, though this will require you give notice to your tenant, and then spend time and money on new paint, carpets, and whatever else the property needs to command top dollar.

Discuss your options with your listing agent, as she will have a good feel for the local market and can advise you on the best course of action.

LISTING AGENT

After making the decision to sell, your first task is to hire the right listing agent, the person who will list your property on MLS and find buyers for you. If you originally purchased the property from a turnkey provider, that provider will be able to sell the property for you—especially if you plan to sell to another investor. Otherwise, you'll have to find an agent.

How to find an agent

A major source of agents is referrals from friends, family, or other investors, but don't assume that means he or she is the right agent for the job. Screen such referrals the same way you would any agent you find online.

My preferred way of finding an agent is to go on real estate websites such as Realtor.com, Zillow, Trulia, and Redfin and search for properties similar to yours. What you're looking for is an agent who is the most active in your geographical area and in your asset class. If you're selling a high-end home in an exclusive area, find out which agents have the most listings for high-end homes in that area. Those are the ones who will have a pipeline of buyers for your type of property.

War Story

Back in the 1990s, there was an agent in Silicon Valley who seemed to be in every newspaper real estate section, every online banner ad, and every milk carton. She called herself "Peggy, Queen of the Condos" and she was everywhere. She specialized in Silicon Valley condos and seemed to know everyone who was either selling or buying a condo. Condos were all she did. If I'd had a condo for sale in Silicon Valley back then, who do you think I'd list it with?

Once you've identified a short list of potential agents, one thing you could do is drop by one of her open houses and play phantom customer. Ask her about local market conditions, average days on market (DOM), and if she's seeing many multiple offers. Do you have rapport with her, and do you think you could work with her? If so, get her card and follow-up later.

Things to know about your prospective agent:

- How many years has she been working full-time in this local market? (Some beginning agents start part-time until their business starts to pick up. They're not your best bet.)

- Has she been a top seller in her office, in both up and down markets?

- Does she have a "feel" for the current market? For example, what features would make the property sell quickly? What upgrades, appliances, touches are worth paying for and which ones aren't? Or is it worth spending the money to stage the house (i.e., place rented designer furniture, wall paintings, towels, etc.) to help buyers visualize the house as their home and make the property sell faster?

- Does she think like an investor? What percent of her clients are investors vs. home buyers? Is she an investor herself?

- How does she market her listings—with open houses, video tours, or online advertising? Does she work in an office with lots of agents who could refer home buyers?

- At what price does she recommend you list the property, and why? Some agents use unrealistically high prices ("Sure, I can get you that price…") in order to entrap unsuspecting sellers, and then fail to perform. A good agent would find what similar properties are selling for, list it at a median price, and start a bidding war to get the price up. (Note: She shouldn't have to research these questions and get back to you; she should know off the top of her head what works and what doesn't in her market.)

- How does she prefer to communicate? Phone, text, email? Will she get back to you within a few hours or a few days?

- What is her contract length? The industry standard is for the seller to contract with the agent for six months. If the agent can't sell the house in six months, then the seller is free to find another agent. This, in my view, is too long for an investor. Especially if you're in a hot market, it shouldn't take longer than three months to sell the property. See if you can negotiate the contract term down. A corollary to this is: Don't ask "At what price should we list the property?" but instead ask "What is the ninety-day sale price?"—i.e., at what price should we list it so that it sells within ninety (or fewer) days? Time is money.

- What is her commission? The industry standard is for both the seller's agent and the buyer's agent to earn 3% of the purchase price, and that's usually fine. An exception might be if you had to sell at a bad time, such as a seller's market when there are many properties available and few buyers. In that case, it might make sense for you and your agent to amend the commission schedule. For example, your agent could accept a lower commission of 2.5% so the buyer's agent can make 3.5%. That extra "kicker" would give an incentive to any buyer's agent to show your property to their clients— and show it first. The reason your agent might be open to accepting a lower commission is if it means she can sell the house in a month instead of six months. Time is money for her, too.

MAKE-READY

Before you put your property on the market, you have to clean the carpets, touch up the paint, and maybe replace appliances and fixtures. This process is called "make-ready."

Deciding on your budget

How much money you should put into the rehab depends on who your ultimate buyer is. If you're planning to sell it to another investor who will use it as a rental, it may not make sense to put in "extras" like granite countertops, brushed nickel fixtures, or stainless-steel appliances in the kitchen. Those extras will cost more and won't enable the investor-buyer to raise his rents very much or at all.

On the other hand, if you're planning to sell to an owner-occupant (a home buyer who'll make it his primary residence), then doing a higher-end rehab will enable you to get top dollar for the house. Even then, you want to make sure that every dollar you spend in rehab will add a dollar or more in a higher selling price. Why spend $2,000 on a Jacuzzi if it raises the home value by only $1,000?

Talk with your real estate agent—the one you chose because she's sold lots of houses in your area—about what improvements to the property make financial sense.

DEALING WITH CONTRACTORS

Your property manager and your realtor should each have a team of licensed and vetted contractors who can help get your property ready for sale. If you find yourself in a situation in which you have to hire contractors yourself, you're in for a challenge.

Competence

I've worked with landscapers who didn't know landscaping and with floor tile installers who didn't know how to install floor tiles. Many contractors will say anything to get the bid and will try to figure it out later. That approach may have worked for them in the past, but it's not going to work with you. You don't want to be the guinea pig for a guy who is learning on the job.

A guy who does hardwood floors may think he can figure out how to do luxury vinyl tile flooring, but he can't. Even the kind of saws needed to cut the tiles are different from the ones used for hardwood.

Reliability

Some contractors will take your deposit, then not show up for the job—and not even call. It turns out, he got another job over the weekend so he went to that one first and will swing by your property whenever he gets around to it. This is surprisingly common.

There's something about the building trades that attracts a certain type of personality: someone who doesn't like to be told what to do (and therefore goes into business for himself) and who comes and goes as he pleases without any sense of obligation to do what he says or communicate. It's literally unbelievable how some of these guys stay in business, but they do.

Expect to babysit ALL contractors until they prove to you that they don't need babysitting.

Fraud

Fraud is another big problem with contractors. Your interior designer might have picked a beautiful granite countertop and back splashes, but it turns out the contractor has some leftover counters from a previous job, so he uses those instead, even though the patterns clash with the back splashes and the color isn't what you picked out. Being clueless about aesthetics himself, he figured he could just use the old counters, pocket the money you advanced him for counters, and no one would notice.

Are you going to spend $3,000 in lawyer fees and three months in small claims court to get the contractor to install the correct counters? I don't think so. The contractor doesn't think so either, so he'll get away with it. He's gotten away with it before.

Bottom line: Assume every contractor and vendor is suspect until they prove otherwise. And the way they prove otherwise is by doing something that's not in their interest but is in your best interest. An example would be a roofer who tells you the whole roof doesn't need to be replaced, only a few shingles. He's talking himself out of a lucrative job, but he's telling you what you need to know. Keep him on your list of good contractors.

POST-SALE

After you sell your property, remember to cancel all the automatic payments you've set up! This includes the HOA dues automatically deducted from your bank account as well as insurance policies. Mortgage payments are not usually a problem because your bank knows you sold the property.

PART II

SPECIAL SITUATIONS

Everything we spoke about in Part I still applies, but now we will present important considerations with special property types.

CHAPTER 12
NEW CONSTRUCTION HOMES

M any investors think that because a house is brand-spanking new, investing in it is a no-brainer—i.e., not much due diligence is required. Not so! Following are a baker's dozen of pitfalls that can happen even with a newly constructed home.

1: GET AN INSPECTION

Mistakes in home construction can happen, and the sooner they're identified and remedied, the better. Example: I bought a new house in Albuquerque in which the water lines were mixed, so the cold-water faucet produced hot water and the hot-water faucet produced cold water. This was identified and corrected right away, but imagine the legal liability if a child turned on the cold-water tap and got scalded.

In most municipalities, a new home has to go through several city inspections during the construction process and also at the end to get a "certificate of occupancy" from the city—meaning the house passed all its inspections and is ready for habitation.

There are several reasons why you should have the new home inspected anyway. First, the city inspector is interested primarily in safety and compliance to building code; he may not notice if there's enough hot water or the A/C doesn't cool the house sufficiently. Secondly, many home builders use multiple subcontractors, and the quality of work can vary from subcontractor to subcontractor, especially when rushing to complete work under a deadline.

In fact, I would argue that instead of not having inspection at all you should actually have two inspections: one when the property is newly built and a second one at around the eleven-month mark. This is because most homebuilders have a twelve-month warranty on their homes and if you can identify any issues at around the eleven-month mark you might be able to get them fixed by the homebuilder for free.

For example, after the house has been lived in for a while, the tenants may notice some things that aren't working quite properly, or maybe the house has settled and there are cracks in the walls or in the foundation. These are things that can be addressed by the homebuilder at no expense to you.

2: WATCH OUT FOR HIDDEN COSTS

A lot of times investors will buy a new home and then after closing find out they have to spend an extra $10,000 out-of-pocket because the new home didn't include things like a fence, sod for the backyard, appliances, or window blinds.

This is not a good surprise. You should always read the purchase contract carefully or ask the builder rep to itemize what is and what is not included in the purchase price. Even within the same market and the same city, what's included in a new-construction home can vary from builder to builder. Anything that needs to be added such as fencing, grass, blinds, or appliances should be added to the purchase price and amortized over the thirty-year loan rather than paid out-of-pocket at closing.

In the previous example of the $10,000 of extra out-of-pocket expenses, if that were included in a thirty-year loan at a 5% interest rate, it would add about $50 to the monthly mortgage. For most investors it's better to pay $50 a month (or have the tenant pay it) than to have to pay the $10,000 up front. Always be aware of what is and is not included in your purchase contract.

3: Ensure There Is a Limit on the Number of Rentals in Your Development

In 2008 right before the financial crisis, some investors purchased properties in new developments in Phoenix, and then discovered that almost the entire development was sold to investors by a builder who was looking to cash out just before the crash! Every other house in the development had a "For Rent" sign outside, which made it hard for the investor to find tenants and didn't help his property values or his rents.

Always make sure there is a limited number of units able to be sold to investors. A good level would be 10% or less (or 20% at most). Also make sure you get this assurance in writing like in the purchase contract, because some builder reps will say anything to make the sale, or they might bend the rules because they want to close out all the houses for sale by year-end. Ideally a limit on the number of rentals in a new development would be in the deed restrictions for the subdivision; in other words, the city planning commission authorized the building of the subdivision with the requirement that only so many of the houses would be made available to investors. That's about as solid a guarantee as you can get.

4: Don't Go Crazy with Builder Upgrades

Sometimes investors will buy a new home and then the builder rep gets them all excited and talks them into extensive upgrades—e.g., granite countertops, subway tile backsplashes, satin nickel finishes, or tiled baths. Each upgrade sounds good and none seems to cost that much by itself, but the total shoots up very quickly, adding 10% to 15% to the cost of the house. The problem is that these upgrades may not raise the rental value of the home: a house in a given neighborhood will only rent for so much.

On the plus side, even if your upgrades don't increase your rents, they might make your property rent faster. Imagine prospective tenants house shopping on a Saturday afternoon and all the $1,500-a-month houses look pretty much the same, but yours really stands out because of its attractive upgrades. You as the investor should weigh the incremental cost of upgrades versus the incremental benefit and decide which way to go.

In addition, you should take advantage of any builder incentives. For example, some builders offer free upgrades or reduced closing costs if you use their lender.

5: Be Cautious with Infill Locations in Older Neighborhoods

So far we talked about new construction in new development subdivisions, but sometimes you get an opportunity to build a new house in an infill location, which is an empty lot in an already established neighborhood.

The danger here is that your new house will not fit in with the neighborhood, especially if it's a really old neighborhood and the older, lower-priced homes around it will cause your property's value to decline. This is the opposite of what most investors prefer to do, which is to buy the worst house in the best neighborhood, then renovate it to bring it up to the neighborhood's standard and realize some forced appreciation.

The key is to make sure that your infill builds are in neighborhoods that are relatively new or affluent. As a rule of thumb, any neighborhood built in 2000 or after is probably okay; in fact, there are a lot of such locations from the 2008 financial crisis, when builders abruptly stopped building in 2008, leaving many available lots in already established subdivisions. If you can get one of those lots and build the house, it will fit in and your property value should align with the neighborhood.

There are other opportunities with affluent neighborhoods. Some older cities like Philadelphia have sections like Society Hill where Betsy Ross's house is; those homes were built in the 1700s! Still, that neighborhood is very exclusive and upscale, and if you were to find an empty lot and build a new home there, your value will be protected because it's in an area surrounded by historical landmarks.

Bottom line: Ask yourself if the surrounding homes help or hurt your new-construction home value.

6: CONSTRUCTION DELAYS

If the construction of your new home is time sensitive, e.g., if you're doing a 1031 exchange (see Glossary) or you want the property completed by the spring so you can find tenants over the summer, then you have to be mindful of construction delays.

Sometimes due to bad weather or other delays, a property that's supposed to be done by March isn't completed until July or August. If you're doing a 1031 exchange, that delay could cause you to miss your 180-day deadline and the IRS will disallow your 1031 exchange, leaving you with a large tax liability. Or, if your home isn't put on the rental market until after the summer, you will have missed the prime renting season.

Once the builder rep gives you the scheduled completion date of the property, add a few months to give yourself some wiggle room. In my experience, construction delays happen about 90% of the time.

7: Don't be HOA-averse

Some investors avoid new construction altogether because they don't want to deal with homeowners associations (HOAs). It's true that sometimes HOAs can be a pain to deal with, but in the long run they can help protect your investment.

Sometimes HOAs cover common area maintenance like lawns and snow removal; they can prevent the neighborhood from having "For Rent" signs; they can prevent houses from being used for short-term rentals like Airbnb; they even make it easier to manage tenants because you can make the HOA the bad guy when enforcing rules—i.e., prompting the tenants to behave more like owners by keeping them in line and making them treat the property as if it were their own.

So rather than categorically rejecting HOAs, you should read the covenants, conditions, and restrictions (CC&Rs) thoroughly; if you can live with the terms, feel free to invest with the HOA in place.

8: Always Visit the Property

Some busy investors think that because the property is new, they don't need to fly out and inspect it personally. That approach can cause problems. Here are some surprises you may experience if you don't visit the property and pick it out yourself:

You buy a property sight unseen and then find out that it's one of the first houses built on the street, so there's lots of construction noise, dug-up streets, workers everywhere, etc., making it difficult to attract tenants.

Not all new homes are created equal! Some houses may be located near power lines; some are on corner lots and have a lot more street traffic and noise; some lots have better views than others and are therefore more desirable. If you're the builder rep, to whom are you going to sell the less-desirable houses—the investors who fly in from out of town, or the investors who buy remotely?

Don't think you can view the house address on Google Maps, because the house has just been built and Google won't have been updated yet! You can only do so much from your desktop. Nothing replaces going there in person to see the development and pick the property you want.

If it's really impossible for you to do a site visit, the next best thing is to ask your property management company to visit the site and take a detailed video tour of the property room-by-room. That means close-ups of fixtures, tiles, cabinets, appliances, and overall layout. Additionally, they should video up-and-down the street and recommend which house and which location would be best for attracting tenants.

One way or the other, someone should visit the property in person; if not you, then your property manager or someone else looking out for your interests.

9: CONSIDER THE PHASES OF CONSTRUCTION

Most new developments are built in phases because the developer doesn't want to put 100 houses on the market all at the same time, and also because the developer needs to sell some houses in Phase I in order to raise the capital to pay for the construction of Phase II.

Here's how the phases work. Let's say a development of sixty houses is being built. The developer will build and "release" the first twenty houses in Phase I, the second twenty houses in Phase 2, and the last twenty houses in Phase 3. Each phase takes three-to-six months, so this development would be sold within one or two years.

There are almost always price increases with each phase, so if you're lucky enough to get in on Phase 1 you might enjoy some appreciation, as the house you bought in Phase I is now selling for $20,000 more by Phase 3.

Thus, factor the construction phase into your purchase decision, but don't let it run your investment decision for you.

Some investors sabotage themselves by never buying in Phase 3, which could be a mistake as well. They are determined not to buy in Phase 3 because they've "missed out" on the potential appreciation, so they'd rather wait until they can get in on Phase 1 of next year's development.

But guess what? Next year's Phase 1 will be more expensive than Phase 3 this year, and you could have gotten the same property this year for less. So don't try to game the system too much. If you find a good property in a good development and the numbers work, it could be a worthwhile investment even though it's in Phase 3. Sometimes, builders will offer special deals because they want to close out the development before the end of the year, and you might be able to take advantage of it.

10: Get Quality Tenants

This is true for all investment properties, but especially true for new builds. It's really disheartening to see a brand-new construction home that's been trashed by bad tenants or pets after one or two years. My advice is to give your property manager permission to wait for the right tenant. During certain times of year—e.g., around the holidays—it's hard to find tenants, given that few people move during Thanksgiving, Christmas, or New Year's, and property managers tend to let anyone in just to keep it occupied. That is a short-term fix that can be a long-term mistake. The quality of the tenant should equal the quality of the home. Give your property manager permission to wait for the right tenant.

Dogma Alert!

I personally would not allow pets in a brand-new construction home. With existing, renovated homes pets are fine, but with new construction there's more downside than upside from allowing pets, in my opinion. Of course, much depends on how "hot" the market for rentals is in your area.

11: BEWARE OF OVERBUILDING IN YOUR MARKET

Back in 2008, some markets like Miami and San Diego were deluged with new condos and houses coming on the market all at the same time, causing prices to plummet. The problem is that developers have a long lead time: It takes years to get building permits from city planning commissions, then hire the general contractors (GCs) to do the actual construction. By the time the properties get on the market, the market may have turned. In 2008 the problem was that the banks just weren't lending to home buyers, so there were too many homes and too few cash buyers, and prices dropped.

This is especially a concern in smaller markets. If you're looking to buy in a small, remote city like Sebring, Florida (population 10,000), it wouldn't take many new homes to simultaneously hit the market to cause a glut and flatten out prices. Home builders are very sensitive to this and will time their release of new homes, so it's something to be aware of.

One resource for determining new housing inventory is to go to NewHomeSource.com, type in the ZIP code or the city name where your property is being built and see how many other brand-new homes are hitting the market at the same time.

Referring back to the example in Exhibit 3.3, we can see that there are 411 new homes for sale in Huntsville, Alabama, of which only sixty are move-in ready. In a metro of 500,000 people, that number of new homes is not going to make a difference. That market is nowhere near being saturated.

If you click on the Find Homes button, you can get more detail on which builders are building, how many homes they are building, and the price ranges. You can see in the lower right-hand corner that most of the homes being built in Huntsville are in the $300,000 range, so if you're buying a $150,000 rental property, these new homes are not competing with you.

Another source of such information is the municipal planning commission for whatever metro you're thinking of investing in. Just Google "[City] Planning Commission" and "[City Name]" and see if you can find information on the number of new housing permits issued. You might also visit that city's Chamber of Commerce site or find realtors in that market online and ask them what's happening on the ground.

12: Research the Most Popular/Practical Floor Plans

You will have the best chance of leasing and eventually selling your property if it has a very popular and desirable floor plan. We discussed a few of these in Chapter 7, such as buying only single-story homes in areas with large retiree populations. The home builder sales rep and your property manager can give you valuable insights into what floor plans and what features (granite counters, stainless appliances, et al.) help get the property rented.

Ask the builder rep "What's your most popular model?" Ask your property manager "Which of these plans would be easiest to rent?" You'll make your property manager's life easier if you get her input before buying.

13: Price Negotiation

Some investors wonder if home prices can be negotiated in a new development, and generally the answer is "no." Here's the problem: Let's say a development has 100 new homes and, in the first phase, the developer drops his price $10,000 from $200,000 to $190,000. That lower price now sets a new (and lower) "comp" for the neighborhood, so the developer doesn't just lose $10,000; he loses $10,000 on each of his 100 houses, or $1,000,000.

Some possible workarounds:

If it's mid-December and there are three houses left and the builder wants to close out the development by year-end, he might be more flexible—though he must be sensitive to jeopardizing the value of previously sold homes. He might consider an arrangement in which you pay the full asking price of $200,000 but he'll give you back $10,000 at closing. In this way, you effectively pay $190,000 for the house but, on the books, it looks like you paid the full $200,000.

Another workaround might be for the builder to keep the price the same, but throw in some upgrades like granite countertops, satin nickel fixtures, stainless appliance package for the kitchen, etc.

Anytime you can find a new-construction home that breaks even or cash flows, that's a good potential investment. New homes rent quickly—more so in this era of Covid-19—because they require minimal maintenance, and you can subsequently sell them within seven to ten years to get out before maintenance starts becoming an issue.

CHAPTER 13
CONDOS

DEFINITIONS

A condominium is a building that's been divided into several units—like apartments—except that the units are sold to individual owners and each unit has its own deed or title.

The primary difference between a condo and a townhome is the land: In a condo, the owner doesn't own the land under the building whereas the owner does in a townhome. In a condo, the owner is responsible for only the space inside the unit (including interior walls). Common areas such as an elevators, pools, parking spaces, and external walls belong to all of the unit owners jointly and are maintained through monthly association dues.

So, do condos make good investment properties? As with anything else, there are pros and cons.

PROS OF A CONDO INVESTMENT

Condos are more affordable

In general, condos cost less than other types of real estate, such as single-family homes or townhomes in the same neighborhood. For a beginning investor with limited capital, a condo might be the easiest entry point into real estate. Given the amount of down payment required for each, the investor's choice might come down to either buying a condo this year or having to wait several years to buy a single-family home.

Even if the investor has sufficient down payment, another scenario is when an investor has low cash reserves. Condos might be a good option for such an investor since the HOA is responsible for big-ticket items.

Desirable locations

Condos are common in trendy "urban core" locations that are popular with millennials. These locations offer "walkability"— the ability to shop, dine, or go to the gym all within walking distance of the condo—and an overall attractive lifestyle. Condos in these areas appeal to white-collar professionals with decent salaries who make good tenants. A detached home in the same area would be prohibitively expensive for an investor to buy and rent to a tenant.

Amenities

Another benefit of condos is amenities such as a pool, Jacuzzi, tennis court, and fitness center.

Residents can enjoy the convenience of not having to travel from home to get exercise, and the time savings are a huge benefit. Occasionally, you can find a condo complex that offers licensed onsite daycare. For many busy tenants, that convenience is the difference between being able to maintain a healthy lifestyle and not. These onsite amenities aren't available to most single-family home tenants, which makes the condo desirable to many prospective tenants.

Security

Most condo complexes have some kind of security, such as roving patrol cars or electronic keys to access the property. Each unit has an intercom that residents can use to "buzz in" visitors or keep unwanted solicitors out. This added security makes residents feel safer.

Fewer maintenance hassles

As the owner of a condo, you're not responsible for common area maintenance like mowing the lawns or clearing snow, as those are the responsibility of the association. The association can do these things on a large scale, more cost-effectively than individual property owners can do on their own.

Condo rules can preserve your investment property's value

Condo rules and regulations can be a pain (see below) but the plus side is that those rules can help preserve your property's value. They prevent owners from painting their front doors a hideous color, using their units for short-term rentals like Airbnb, storing trash on the balconies, or making too much noise.

These restrictions keep the development a desirable place to live and prevent you, the owner, from being at the mercy of your least-considerate neighbor. And when your tenant steps out of line, it's much easier to make the HOA the "bad guy" and blame the restrictions on the HOA.

CONS OF CONDO INVESTMENT

Homeowners association fees

HOA fees can range from under $100 to as much as $500 per month depending on the location, age, and quality of the community. These fees also go up every year with the cost of inflation, usually around 5%. Some association bylaws limit the amount that HOA fees can go up each year, but that doesn't always protect you.

In certain situations, you may get hit with a one-time "special assessment," which is an additional fee assessed on all owners for a special project, like repaving the parking lot, or paying the deductible for unexpected damage from a hailstorm. As an owner, you have no control over these assessments.

As condo complexes get older (say, fifteen years or more), HOA expenses might start growing faster than rents, in which case your cash flow is going to suffer. Imagine if rents are going up 2.5% per year ($25 on a $1,000/month rental) but expenses are growing 5% per year. Nothing good can come from that trend.

Finally, when you eventually decide to sell the property, high HOA fees can turn off prospective buyers. Buyers can accept principal and interest payments of $700 per month, but they balk at paying an additional $300 or more per month for HOA fees.

Condos can be harder to finance—both when you buy and when you sell

Lenders have tougher underwriting requirements for a condo than for a detached single-family home, because not only do you, the buyer, have to qualify for the loan, but the condo association has to as well.

A conventional lender will generally lend only if the development is at least 50% owner-occupied, has a homeowners association with a low delinquency rate (namely, owners who are behind on their dues payments), and no ongoing litigation. If any of these criteria are not met, you will not be able to get a conventional loan.

Worse still, if you do get the loan and then years later these criteria are no longer met when you're trying to sell your property, your potential buyers will not be able to get a loan either. If this happens, you'll either be stuck with the property when you want to sell it, or your pool of potential buyers will be limited to only cash buyers, and those cash buyers will make only low-ball offers.

Less appreciation

In general, condos appreciate in value at a much slower rate than detached homes. This is because the owner owns only the living space inside of the unit and not the land under it. In real estate, much of appreciation comes from the value of the land.

HOA Rules and Restrictions

Some HOAs act like they own the property, not you. They nitpick every little thing—like how far your SUV extends beyond your carport or what items you store on the balcony. Following are some restrictions you should research before buying a condo as an investment property.

Can your unit be rented?

Most HOAs allow renting, but some do not. Those that do have rental caps—i.e., they impose a limit on the percentage of condos in the development that can be rented to third-party tenants, for example 25% of the units. If the condo development you're considering has already met its rental cap, you the owner will have to put your name on a waiting list before you can rent out your unit. In addition, some HOAs allow owners to rent their condos only after they've owned them for at least one year.

Make sure you get a copy of the association's Covenants, Conditions & Restrictions (CC&Rs) and study it carefully to determine what you can and cannot do.

Other restrictions

Aside from rental policies, there are other rules such as what colors you can paint the exterior doors, where guests can park, and if pets are allowed (including how many pets, and what size!). Make a reader-friendly version of all these restrictions and have prospective tenants read and agree to abide by them.

The HOA usually has no legal authority to enforce its rules on third parties, such as tenants. But if your tenant doesn't abide by the association's rules, the HOA does have the authority to take action against you, the landlord. Make sure your tenant understands and agrees to whatever rules are in place.

HOA (MIS)MANAGEMENT

One thing investors rarely think of is whether or not the HOA is competent and managing the community well. When you submit your offer, you should get a copy of current audited financial documents from the HOA. Here are some things to look out for:

Does the HOA have a strong balance sheet?

Does it have funds in reserve, either in CDs or other instruments easily convertible to cash?

Have reserves been set up and earmarked for anticipated major expenses, like a new roof or repaving the parking area?

Delinquencies

What percent of the owners are delinquent in paying their HOA dues? How many have been delinquent for multiple months?

Revenues vs. expenses

Related to delinquencies, looking at the financials by month, are expenses growing faster than revenues? If so, an increase in HOA fees is likely and you should factor that in to your cash flow projections for the property.

Aside from the financials, how well is the HOA managing the lawns, the pool, and other common areas? Is the property maintained as a desirable place to live?

Go to Yelp.com and see what kind of reviews the HOA is getting from existing owners. Is the HOA responsive when there's an issue?

Dogma Alert!

I personally have never invested in condos. I would consider doing so only if I could buy (a) primarily for equity growth (i.e., in a neighborhood that's appreciating rapidly); (b) in a development that's under five years old (that's old enough for me to see the HOA's financial and operational track record, but not old enough to have high HOA fees yet); or (c) with fewer than 25% of the units as rentals and HOA fee delinquencies under 5% per year (so I'll have buyers when I go to sell it in a few years, before the HOA fees get too onerous).

CHAPTER 14

SMALL MULTIFAMILIES
(2-4 UNITS)

We now turn our discussion to the 2-4-unit multifamilies, which are considered "residential" (not commercial) by Fannie/Freddie. An investor can get a conventional loan for 2-4 units as easily as for a single-family home.

PROS OF MULTIFAMILY PROPERTIES

Economies of scale

It's easier to manage one fourplex than to manage four single-family homes (management).

It's cheaper to replace one roof every twenty years than four roofs every twenty years (expenses).

It's faster to reach a passive income target (e.g., $5,000 per month in passive income) with five fourplexes than with twenty single-family homes.

Maximize loans

As mentioned previously, the lending agencies Fannie Mae/ Freddie Mac will allow conventional financing for up to ten properties per investor. If an investor is limited to ten loans, then by buying ten fourplexes, the investor can own forty doors instead of just ten. This is very appealing, especially to cash flow investors. If the investor's spouse has a W-2 job and can qualify for a loan, then the household could have twenty properties, and twenty fourplexes would yield eighty doors, not just twenty.

Stepping stone

Many investors want to eventually invest in larger apartment buildings of twelve, twenty, or fifty or more units, but it's a big leap from a single-family home to a fifty-unit apartment building. For many, getting a fourplex is a gateway into the world of multifamily, a way of dipping one's toe in the water and gaining experience in that asset class, as well as demonstrating to a commercial lender of 5+ unit properties that the investor is a credible borrower for that asset class.

Dogma Alert!

Personally, I would rather own ten fourplexes than one forty-unit apartment building. Owning a forty-unit building is easier to manage, but then you lose diversification. You basically have all your eggs in one basket. Suppose you own a forty-unit apartment complex and the city passes a rent control law? You're stuck. With ten fourplexes, you could diversify by having them in different cities or states.

Finally, another popular strategy for these properties is to "house hack." That means the buyer will buy a fourplex, live in one unit, and rent out the other three. Over time, as the neighborhood improves and rents go up, the investor hopes to live in her unit for free, as the rent from the other three units covers all the owner's expenses. This is a viable option not obtainable from single-family homes.

CONS OF MULTIFAMILY PROPERTIES

Property managers

The property managers who manage 2-4 units are usually single-family home property managers who've moved "up market" to manage small multifamilies. Just make sure their software can track expenses by unit—not just by building—and how they account for common area expenses such as snow removal or lawn care. This is usually not a big deal, as most can do this, but confirm before you buy.

Legal liability

In a single-family home, the tenant is responsible for everything, but in a multifamily, the landlord is often responsible for common areas like hallways, laundry rooms, lawn care, and snow/ice removal. If the hallway smoke detector battery dies, who's liable? If your property manager's snow removal service didn't get to the property in time and your tenant slips on the ice, who's liable?

Regardless of what your lease agreement or property management agreement says, more often than not the tenant will sue the landlord (you) and then you'll have to sue the property manager and/or the snow removal service. This liability is not necessarily a deal-breaker—investors do own multifamily properties and make them work—but it's an issue you should be prepared for.

The way to protect yourself is to over-insure by getting extra liability coverage, and/or holding your property in an LLC. If you go the over-insurance route, a good rule of thumb is to have an additional $300,000 of coverage per door and per occurrence. Ask your insurance agent what makes sense based on what she's seen in your market.

Neighborhoods

With a single-family home in a good ("B" or better) neighborhood, most of the houses on the street are owner-occupied. Most owner-occupants have pride of ownership and take care of their properties, and if you own the one rental on that street, your investment will enjoy the inherent protection of its surroundings.

Multifamilies, however, tend to be in neighborhoods of other multifamilies—e.g., fourplexes or apartment complexes. You may maintain your fourplex very well, but if the slumlord next door lets his property deteriorate with junk on the front lawn, weeds, less-than-desirable tenants, etc., that will affect what quality tenant you can attract and what rents you can command. You can't control that and can't influence the outcome, so you're at the mercy of your fellow landlords on the street.

This is where onsite due diligence and/or virtual video tours are key, before you buy. Make sure you know what the street and surrounding neighborhoods look like, and pay particular attention to the properties closest to the one you're thinking of buying.

Tenant profile

Few people actually prefer to live in a small multifamily. Most renters want either a house where there's a feeling of privacy and ownership, or an apartment in a 100-unit complex where there are amenities like a swimming pool or tennis courts. The small multifamily lacks both the privacy of a single-family home and the amenities of a large complex.

Because of this, in a "C" neighborhood these units often attract lower-quality tenants, with lower credit scores, spotty work history—people who can't generally qualify to rent in an apartment complex.

Tenant turnover

Due to the issues noted above, the 2-4-unit place is often just a stepping stone for many tenants until they can move someplace nicer; thus, tenant turnover for the multifamily owner tends to be higher.

Personality and behavioral issues

In a small multifamily, your tenants may get on each other's nerves: One tenant is playing music too loudly, another leaves bikes in the driveway. Mitigate this by posting clear rules, going over the rules at the time a tenant agrees to rent, and displaying a map showing the common areas vs. those for each tenant only.

Exit strategy

You can always sell a house to either an investor or an owner-occupant. With a multifamily, you're selling only to an investor, which is a much smaller pool of potential buyers. Also, those buyers are looking at it solely as a business decision (purely practical) and will look to bargain. That said, there is strong demand for 2-4-unit multifamilies among investors. Just know that your pool of available buyers is smaller.

Rent control

Rent control legislation is being passed in various states and municipalities around the country. If you own a single-family home, rent control might not be a problem because you could always sell the house on MLS to an owner-occupant at prevailing market values supported by comparable sales ("comps").

With multifamilies however, rent control can limit the amount of income your property can produce. That means when you sell, your property will not be as attractive to potential buyers (who will be investors)—or you might not be able to sell it at all! Some investors hear "rent control" and head for the hills.

VALUATION

Valuation of small multifamily properties is a little trickier than for a house. Multifamilies are considered residential for financing purposes, i.e., you can buy them with the same residential Fannie/Freddie loans you would use for a single-family house so that's how they're valued—as residential.

Note: You can use a commercial loan if you want—e.g., if you've used up your ten Fannie/Freddie loans and have no option but to take out a commercial loan, the appraiser will still value the building as a residential property. In other words, it'll be appraised based on comps—what comparable properties in that neighborhood have sold for recently.

Investors, on the other hand, tend to think of small multifamilies as they would a commercial property: Cash-on-cash returns, net operating income (NOI), and capitalization rates ("cap rates"). Looking at such properties this way is useful for comparing one investment opportunity with another, especially against a commercial property like a warehouse or office building.

Here's the gotcha: Suppose you buy a fourplex, renovate it, raise the rents, and increase the net operating income of the property and make it more profitable than when you bought it. The appraiser will still appraise it based on comps (what other fourplexes in the neighborhood have sold for) even though those fourplexes aren't as profitable as yours.

So the standard commercial strategy of buying a property and forcing appreciation by increasing its NOI may not have much effect on how much you can sell it for. You may have bought the fourplex for $400,000, raised its net operating income hoping to sell it for $500,000, and find out that it's still valued at close to $400,000. All that hard work for nothing!

The same is true if you try to do a cash-out refinance ("refi"): The bank will likely treat it as a $400,000 property, not a $500,000 property.

If your strategy is to buy a multifamily, fix it up, and increase its value, you have to be careful not to over-improve the property. The way to do this is to think in reverse: Given that the "comps" for fourplexes in this neighborhood is $400,000, what's the most I can afford to pay for the property in the first place ($300,000?), and what's the most I can afford in my rehab budget ($50,000?) and still come out ahead with an end-valuation of $400,000?

ADDITIONAL DUE DILIGENCE STEPS

Typically, you won't be able to see the inside of the unit until *after* you've submitted an offer and it's been accepted. This is because sellers don't want to inform their tenants that the property is for sale or hassle their tenants with showings by a dozen prospective buyers. They'll only risk alerting the tenants when they know the buyer is "for real" and they have a signed contract.

This is somewhat of a catch-22. How can you negotiate price or terms before you've seen the inside of the units and their condition? The seller will usually have photos left over from the last time he had the units up for rent, so that's a start. Or if you're close to making an offer, you can ask the property manager to do some "maintenance" on each unit, like check the smoke detectors, air filters, etc. and assess the state of the units that way.

To protect yourself, make sure the purchase contract gives you, the buyer, the option to cancel the sale without penalty after the units have been inspected by a licensed inspector.

Why is the seller selling?

When a small multifamily comes on the market, you have to wonder why it's being sold. If this property were a cash cow for the owner, he likely wouldn't be selling it. If a broker/agent has a great deal, he'd offer it to his core list of special clients first, and to the clients of other agents in his real estate office second.

Unless you are on a broker's "short list" of special clients, the only properties you're likely to see on MLS are the ones that their favorite investors have passed on. So when a small multifamily comes on the market, it is wise to proceed with caution.

In any market you're considering, the key is to talk to property managers and ask them if these small apartments work in her market and where in her market they work best.

STRATEGIES FOR 2-4 MULTIFAMILIES

Neighborhoods

In some cities like San Francisco, you can get a Victorian and divide it into 2-3 units and they work because they're in good neighborhoods and can attract quality tenants. In a city where the average home is $1.5M, many MBAs and attorneys are renters!

Turnover

One way to minimize the tenant turnover problem is to strategically over-improve the units above what tenants expect in a rental (granite countertops, brushed nickel fixtures, stainless-steel appliances, etc.) and keep the rents about the same *for the good tenants*. The tenants know that for the same rent, they're unlikely to get anything comparable and so they'll stay.

Another option is to sign only two-year leases in the first lease term. With the cost of vacancy (loss of a month's rent, plus make-ready, advertising, and leasing costs) it may not even be profitable to rent to a tenant for one year. So why do it? Sign an initial two-year lease (making it worth your while) and offer one-year renewals after that. That way you're setting yourself up to make money. You may lose some applicants, but others will agree to it so they can "lock in" the rent for two years. Your property manager can help get you a two-year lease by asking them "Do you really want to pack and move again after only one year?"

Tip

Be especially careful with your tenant screening if you go with a two-year lease. If you get a marginal tenant, you might be stuck with him for two years. Great tenants are obviously preferred, and terrible tenants can be evicted, but the marginal ones can become the proverbial thorn-in-the-side.

Another factor is to get the right type of property. If you get a building with all one-bedroom, one-bath units, you'll attract a transient tenant who will outgrow the unit and move. If you have two-bedroom or three-bedroom units, you can attract couples or starter families who tend to be more stable.

Screening tenants

One reason for high turnover is that property management companies fill multifamily vacancies the same way they fill single-family home vacancies: They take applications, run criminal and credit checks, then approve the tenant. This is a mistake in my view. In a multi-family, you need to take the additional step of considering the compatibility of the tenants to each other. One reason for high turnover is that one tenant is noisy (loud music) and the other likes quiet; one tenant has cats and the other is allergic to cats. The close confines of living "on top of each other" creates an additional dimension your property manager should incorporate into the process—which many property managers don't have time to do. They just want to find bodies to fill vacancies and move on to the other thousand things they have to do each day.

Discuss this with your property manager. Pay extra tenant placement fees if you have to. Give her permission to take longer to find the right tenant rather than fill the vacancy with the first body that comes along.

ADDITIONAL CONSIDERATIONS

Have a storage area

If the layout of the property allows, it's best to have a storage area where the tenants can store bikes, boxes, sporting goods, etc.—or they'll be stored on your lawn.

Publish rules

Post rules about how quickly clothes should be removed from the washer/dryer so others can use them; where the trash bins are to be placed and how soon they need to be taken inside after trash day; where sports equipment like basketball hoops may/may not be situated.

Keep rents for comparable units about the same

Your tenants will eventually wind up talking with each other, and if one tenant is paying significantly more than another for a two-bedroom, one-bath unit, that will cause you problems unless you can show why one unit should cost more (such as nicer finishes). And a tenant's idea of "significant" might be $20/month, so it's their definition of "significant" you have to consider, not yours.

When multifamilies work, they cash flow really well, so if you venture into the multifamily space, do your due diligence up front and give it your best shot.

CONCLUSION

The previous chapters gave you a road map for how to do due diligence on your potential real estate investments: Identify good markets—either on your own or through a turnkey provider—then evaluate the neighborhoods, properties, property managers and pro formas—and start investing!

What we've covered in this book may seem overwhelming, but don't be discouraged. Remember that you'll have experts to guide you through most of the process: your agent or turnkey provider, your lender, your property manager and others.

What you as the investor have to focus on is choosing the right market, evaluating neighborhoods—especially if done remotely—and sanity-checking the pro forma financial statements. If you can get comfortably doing those three things, your team of experts can help you with the rest.

At this point, there's only one due diligence category left to discuss, namely due diligence on yourself: *Are you, personally, cut out to be a real estate investor?*

TIME FLEXIBILITY

While buy-and-hold investing shouldn't take more than a few hours a week, at times it can take more, such as when you have a tenant turn, or when something breaks down. You have to be available to work with your property manager and give her direction.

This might be my imagination, but when problems do arise, they always seem to happen at the worst possible time—e.g., a tenant's roof will spring a leak on the day before you go on family vacation. It's Murphy's Law. You have to be able to laugh and roll with the punches.

PRUDENT INVESTMENT DECISIONS

Have sufficient reserves to pay for unexpected expenses so one bad situation doesn't take you down. Don't leverage yourself to the hilt with risky interest-only or adjustable-rate mortgages (ARMs). In the Covid-19 era, how many tenants could stop paying rent without you getting negative cash flow? You have to play defense as well as offense.

TEMPERAMENT

Real estate investing is a business, and you can't get emotionally involved in it. When problems arise—and they will—you can't afford to lose sleep over it. You have to learn to *reduce every challenge to a math problem.*

Let's imagine that you've evicted a tenant and, out of spite, he poured concrete down the toilet and disappeared in the middle of the night. It happens. What are you going to do? Grow an ulcer? Lie awake at night planning "the perfect crime"?

Get a repair estimate. Tell your property manager to pay for the bulk of the repairs out of the tenant's security deposit. Have the plumbing inspected and get the place rented and cash flowing quickly.

Treat it like a math problem.

If you have the temperament, manage your business conservatively, and can roll with the punches, you could have a career in real estate investing, and this book can help you get on your way.

I'll end this book at the same place it started:

"If you follow the guidelines in this book to the letter,
you will never buy an investment property in your lifetime."

No property is going to check all the boxes and provide you with the textbook investment opportunity. All investing involves tradeoffs—between appreciation and cash flow, between risk and reward, between booming markets that might bust vs. stable markets that don't do either.

The guidelines in this book are just a tool to help you analyze what you're getting into, weigh the pros and cons of each investment opportunity, and help you decide which risks you're willing to take vs. those you aren't.

I hope you found this book worthwhile and it helps you succeed as a real estate investor.

Happy Investing,
Joe Torre

APPENDIX A - GLOSSARY

1031 Exchanges

The 1031 Exchange is a provision in the tax code that allows you to sell one or more appreciated investment properties (called the "relinquished property") and defer the payment of your capital gains taxes by acquiring one or more like-kind properties (called the "replacement properties").

Appraisal

A determination of the value of something, such as a house. A professional appraiser—a qualified, disinterested expert—makes an estimate by examining the property, as well as looking at the initial purchase price and comparing it with recent sales of similar property. Banks use appraisals to confirm the worth of real estate for lending purposes, and insurance companies require appraisals to determine the amount of damage done to covered property before settling insurance claims.

Appraised Value

An estimate of the present worth of a property, made by a state-licensed appraiser.

After-Repair-Value (ARV)

After-repair-value is the value of a property after it's been renovated. For example, an investor might buy a house for $100,000 and put $40,000 worth of renovations and upgrades into it. Once done, its After-Repair-Value (ARV) might be $200,000. The investor is banking on the likelihood that the ARV will be significantly higher than the acquisition and renovation costs, so he can make a profit.

Bird Dogs

In real estate, a "bird dog" is slang for someone who finds properties for investors. The bird dog could be one of several agents that you asked to keep an eye out for certain types of properties, or even a teenager with a bicycle who roams neighborhoods looking for properties that fit your criteria and takes pictures of them with his cell phone. The expression comes from hunting dogs that point to the location of downed birds.

Broker's Price Opinion (BPO)

A broker's price opinion (BPO) is the estimated value of a property as determined by a real estate broker who estimates a property's value based on an exterior drive-by, knowledge of the neighborhood, and comparison of similar homes in the area. The BPO is not as thorough as an appraisal, which is done by a licensed appraiser and includes an examination of the interior of the property. BPOs are a "first pass" that provides a quick, less expensive, and less time-consuming estimate of value.

Capital Expenditure (CapEx)

In real estate, CapEx refers to funds used to upgrade physical assets to improve the useful life of a property, which cannot be expensed in the current year for tax purposes. Examples would include replacing a roof (depreciated over twenty years) or replacing appliances (depreciated over five years).

Capital Gain

The profit on the sale of a capital asset, such as stock or real estate. If you buy a house for $100,000 and sell it five years later for $150,000, you've realized a $50,000 capital gain.

Capital Gains Tax

The capital gains tax is a tax you pay when you sell an asset that has increased in value since you bought it. For real estate investors holding a property longer than one year, the federal rate is usually 20%. In the previous example, the investor would pay 20% of $50,000, or $10,000 (unless the investor did a 1031 exchange). Each state may also have a capital gains tax at the state level.

Capitalization Rate (Cap rate)

The rate of expected return on investment property without financing. For example, if you buy a property all-cash for $100,000 and you net $10,000 per year in cash flow after all expenses and reserves, your cap rate is 10% ($10,000 divided by $100,000).

Comparables (Comps)

Properties that are similar to a particular property and used to compare and estimate a value for that property. For example, if a house in a certain neighborhood is listed for sale at $100,000, you can go to online real estate sites and look for similar houses (same number of bedrooms, baths, square footage) in the same zip code to see if the listed price of $100,000 is "in the ballpark" for that type of property in that area.

Covenants, Conditions & Restrictions (CC&Rs)

The restrictions governing the use of real estate, usually enforced by a homeowners association and passed on to the new owners of property. For example, CC&Rs may tell you how often you must mow your lawn, what colors you may paint your garage doors, or what kind or size of dog breeds you may have. If property is subject to CC&Rs, buyers must be notified before the sale takes place.

Cash-on-Cash Return (CCR)

Cash-on-cash return is the annual cash flow (before tax) divided by the total cash invested in the property. For example, if a $100,000 property nets $6,000 per year after all expenses, the investor's cash-on-cash return is 6.0%.

Days on Market (DOM)

Days on market is the number of days that a property has been available for sale, from the time it's listed on the local multiple listing service (MLS) until the time a seller has accepted an offer and signed a contract. It can apply to a specific property or describe average days on market for an entire metro area. In a balanced market, homes remain on the market for an average of sixty to ninety days from listing to closing. In a "hot" market, average days on market could be as little as a week or less.

Doors

This is a term used by multifamily investors to indicate how many units a property has. For example, an owner of four fourplexes would have four properties but sixteen "doors." Single-family home investors usually think in terms of properties; multifamily investors think in terms of doors.

Earnest Money Deposit (EMD)

An Earnest Money Deposit is the amount a buyer pays to the seller at the time of entering a purchase contract. It shows that the buyer is serious about buying the property and it gives the seller a reason to take the property off the market while the buyer is arranging financing, inspections, and appraisals. If the buyer breaks the contract, the EMD is kept by the seller as compensation for having taken the property off the market and not entertaining other offers. The EMD amount is usually about $5,000.

Escrow Account

1. A third-party account that holds money while a sale is in progress. An example would be a title company that retains the buyer's Earnest Money Deposit (EMD) to hold the property while the buyer gets a loan approved by a bank.

2. An account used to hold funds required for the payment of a future liability. An example would be a bank's escrow account to pay for the borrower's property taxes, hazard insurance, homeowner's dues, etc.

Homeowners Association (HOA)

An organization that regulates and manages the common areas of a housing subdivision or condominium complex. These associations maintain common areas, and enforce the Covenants, Conditions & Restrictions (CC&Rs) that apply to the property. Property owners are charged monthly dues to pay for the staffing and expenses of the HOA.

Infill Location

An infill location is a vacant lot in an established neighborhood where a new home can be built. For example, when the financial crisis of 2008 occurred, many home builders abruptly stopped building, so there are existing housing subdivisions with vacant lots available for future home sites. These are known as infill locations.

Lease Option

A lease option is a contract in which a landlord and tenant agree that, at the end of a specified period (usually around five years), the tenant can buy the property at a pre-determined price. The tenant pays an up-front option fee and an additional amount each month (usually around 10% of monthly rent) that goes toward the eventual down payment.

This enables a potential home buyer to move into a house she wants to eventually buy without having to come up with a down payment at the outset. If the tenant chooses not to exercise the option to buy, the owner keeps the additional rent paid.

Loan-to-Value Ratio (LTV)

The ratio of the loan amount divided by the appraised value of the property. For example, if the buyer puts $20,000 down on a $100,000 house and takes out an $80,000 loan, the LTV is 80% (=$80,000 / $100,000). Loan-to-value ratios can affect the mortgage interest rate that the buyer pays and whether the buyer can qualify for a loan in the first place, as well as other lender requirements.

Make-Ready

This refers to the process of getting a property ready for sale, or ready to accept a new tenant, and includes such things as cleaning, touching up the paint, putting in new carpets, and anything else the property needs to be made marketable.

Pre-Approval Letter

This is a letter from a bank or other lender, which shows what size loan the borrower qualifies for. Sellers of properties want to see a pre-approval letter from any potential buyer, to ensure that the buyer is "for real" and can actually qualify for a loan.

Principal, Interest, Taxes, and Insurance (PITI)

Principal and interest comprise the mortgage payment on a property. Taxes are property taxes and are paid each year based on the assessed value of the property. Insurance is any insurance held on the property. These four components are the major financial expenses for a homeowner.

Rent Ratio

This is an industry rule of thumb to give investors a quick indicator of whether a property will cash flow or not. It's simply the monthly rent divided by the purchase price. The ideal is to find a property with a 1% rent ratio—e.g., a $100,000 house that rents for $1,000 per month. If a property meets that hurdle, then it's worth the investor's time to do a detailed analysis of expenses to get a more precise estimate of the property's cash potential. Note: When interest rates are low (say, under 5%) even properties with a 0.8% rent ratio can cash flow in some markets.

APPENDIX B –
LIST OF RESOURCES

1031 Exchange Facilitator
Asset Preservation, Inc.
Dino Champagne
Asset Preservation Inc. (Irvine, CA)
dino@apiexchange.com
866-857-1031

Asset Protection/LLCs/Taxes/Estate Planning
Kelly Allison
Senior Business Strategist
Anderson Advisors (Las Vegas, NV)
KAllison@AndersonAdvisors.com
800-706-4741 Ext 265

Insurance
Michelle Pepper
Insurance Agent-Home, Auto, Life
Davis-Dyer-Max, Inc. (Dallas, TX)
michelle.pepper@davis-dyer-max.com
972-864-0400

APPENDIX B – LIST OF RESOURCES

Lenders
Graham Parham
Highlands Mortgage (Dallas, TX)
GParham@HighlandsMortgage.com
855-326-6802

Aaron Chapman
Security National Mortgage Corporation (Phoenix, AZ)
Aaron.Chapman@snmc.com
602-732-3993

Free Investor Education
www.BiggerPockets.com
www.RealWealthNetwork.com
www.Landlordology.com

Market Data
City-Data.com
Niche.com
Neighborhood360.com
GoodSchools.org
NeighborhoodScout.com
CrimeReports.com

CPSIA information can be obtained
at www.ICGtesting.com
Printed in the USA
FSHW021557240521
81774FS